ARIZONA HOAs and ALL THAT JAZZ!

The Ultimate Arizona Guide for Homeowners, Board Members, and Professionals Involved in HOA Management

ADVANCE PRAISE

HOAs and All That Jazz! is a great resource to help potential owners determine whether they really want to take up residence in an HOA. The authors point out that although owners can experience significant benefits, they have responsibilities too, which expectations are shown here. The Sweetows, having experienced HOAs from many viewpoints have not written a one-sided book. It is constructed to serve homeowners, managers, boards and any other professional supporting HOAs in any manner. The couple's credentials are impressive, and there is value in what they have to say. Readers can benefit from the collection of long-range experience, and help many people benefit from participation—at any level—in today's HOAs.

~ TR Stearns
Retired Superintendent of Schools
Former HOA Board Member

ARIZONA HOAs and ALL THAT JAZZ!

The Ultimate Arizona Guide for Homeowners, Board Members, and Professionals Involved in HOA Management

Burton and Susan Sweetow

Arizona HOAs and All That Jazz! should be considered the ultimate reference for Arizona HOA homeowner's, board members and their management—Real Estate agents, investors, attorneys—and anyone considering a purchase in an HOA.

Note: This book contains applicable laws pertaining to HOA as published under the Arizona Revised Statutes.

The law is always in the public domain, whether it consists of government statutes, ordinances, regulations, or judicial decisions.

When a model code is enacted into law, it becomes a fact—the law of a particular local government. Indeed, the particular wording of a law is itself a fact, and that wording cannot be expressed in any other way. A fact itself is not copyrightable, nor is the way that the fact is expressed if there is only one way to express it. Since the legal code of a local government cannot be expressed in any way but as it is actually written, the fact and expression merge, and the law is uncopyrightable.

(Veeck v. Southern Building Code Congress International, Inc., 293 F.3d 791 (5th Cir. 2002).)

DEDICATION

This book is dedicated to our Mother Myrel
who lived past 100 and never lost her passion
for learning or her spirit for justice.

We cannot seek achievement for ourselves and forget about progress and prosperity for our community...
Our ambitions must be broad enough to include the aspirations and needs of others, for their sakes and for our own.

Cesar Chavez (1927-1993)
American Activist

Table of Contents

FOREWORD

───────◆◇◆───────

AS PART OF their unrelenting quest to educate homeowners, HOA boards, management companies, real estate agents, and attorneys regarding the benefits and difficulties of owning property governed by HOAs, the Sweetows have written an educational, informative, and easy-to-understand guidebook—*HOAs and All That Jazz!*, which will be my go-to-guide for many years to come. This book is a must-have for anyone in the real estate industry that I recommend to all of my colleagues. A brilliant piece of work by the Sweetows

~Patrick MacQueen
Real Estate Attorney, Phoenix, AZ

───────◆◇◆───────

THE WORLD IS fortunate to have experienced people step up to the plate and write a book that is at once a great resource, a quick and easy read, and one that is written with great passion and transparency. The authors of *HOAs and All That Jazz!* put pen to paper and tell it like it is—from exposing homeowners being victimized by mismanaged HOAs and providing the very statutes garnered by the State of Arizona—to protect them. They speak of working within the system, yet leave room for those who feel their "issue" with the homeowners association is more than trivial in nature.

I am sure the authors wish they had *HOAs and All That Jazz!* early in their careers and in their own personal home ownership. I am, however, impressed that everyone who has any kind of interest in HOAs will now have a "road map" to understanding and better governance. Far too many HOAs are run by well-intentioned volunteers—who have far too little knowledge not only of what their job functions are, but act and make decisions that are in compliance with rulings of which they are not fully aware. Additionally, far too many HOA boards are not aware of the fiduciary responsibility to its members.

Insightful education is what *HOAs and All That Jazz!* is about! The authors wisely discuss the need for communication that begins with listening, address board meetings that do not turn into hotly contested, draw attention to reserves, maintenance and special assessments, and expose proper management of budget and financial information. All in all, *HOAs and All That Jazz!* should be required reading—for homeowners who understand their vested interest, Board Members who want/need to have a highly-performing HOA, management companies and other professional services that support HOAs at any level.

If you are a reader who has ever wondered what a healthy, well-run HOA could look like, this book has all the essentials necessary to hire a professional management company, create productive and collaborative boards, and oh! so much more. No matter how knowledgeable one may or may not be about HOAs, there is something in *HOAs and All That Jazz!* for everyone; an easy-to-read resource used as a continued reference—adaptable, proven elements for successful HOAs.

Every homeowner is entitled to the peaceful enjoyment of their homes, particularly those who have chosen to reside in communities managed by HOAs. It is the wisdom of these authors to make this goal a little easier for Arizona's homeowners.

PREFACE

WHEN WE DECIDED to write this book, over a year ago, we had no idea that it would consume us!

It came about as a result of discussions on HOAs in our real estate classes. The agents let us know that they felt there should be more information available to them, their clients, HOA boards and homeowners on this subject. They seemed to feel it was a hot issue that was often misunderstood.

So, we decided to write a book and include Arizona Statutes pertinent to the subject!

In it we hope to respond to the many questions students ask of us, and touch the many conversations we had with others over the years—about HOA's, which ran the gamut:

> From... questions about homeowners associations in general, to the legal rights of homeowners living him HOAs;

> From... demanding audits of the HOA records to understanding the "rules"; and

> From... the steps to being an HOA Warrior and taking on an abusive board, to having access to the myriad connections and resources that close the circle in the environments of HOAs.

Here it is—we trust it will be of help to those who are in one way or another, involved in an HOA as a form of government.

ACKNOWLEDGEMENT

WE ACKNOWLEDGE EVERY person who assisted in any manner in the inspiration, writing, and publishing of *Arizona HOAs and All That Jazz!* It has been quite an adventure and we could not have done it without you. We have not added names—the list would be too long. You know who you are and how you supported our project and for that, we are ever grateful.

ARIZONA HOAs and ALL THAT JAZZ!

SECTION I
INTRODUCTION

―――――∾∾∾―――――

*For, usually and fitly, the presence of an
introduction is held to imply that there is
something of consequence and importance to
be introduced.*

~ Arthur Machen (1863-1947)
Welsh Author

―――――∾∾∾―――――

WHO ARE WE
AND WHY DID WE WRITE THIS BOOK?

WE ARE SUSAN Sweetow, Realtor® Emeritus and Burton Sweetow,
Designated Broker. Between us we have over 90 years as Realtors®
and own the Southwestern School of Real Estate, Scottsdale,
Arizona, which was founded in 1989. It is a boutique school that
specializes in continuing education, as approved by the Arizona
Department of Real Estate (ADRE).

We have lived in and owned property in several condominiums
and planned communities, so you would think we had all the
answers. What we discovered, however—we actually possessed what
was an abundance of questions! We wondered why HOAs were so
often thought of as a social club rather than a very serious large
business with huge financial concerns. These simple questions were
in the beginning of our journey to be of help to the vast number of
people entering into contracts with HOAs. People do not always
know what they don't know; our intention is to increase your
awareness, diminish your risk, and answer questions you were not

aware you might have. We will address situations such as the fact that not every homeowner is aware in Arizona—under 33-1260 (A3h) and 33-1806 (A3h)—buyers acknowledge that they have entered into an "enforceable" contract with their HOA.

ARE ALL HOAS CREATED EQUAL?

NOT BY A long shot. Some run efficiently... a few have excellent hardworking self-sacrificing boards, and others have licensed management—many don't! With myriad variances, how can you tell the difference? What do you need to know before purchasing and once a member of a community, what are your rights? Or, did you give up your rights when you entered into a contract with the HOA?

When buying property in Arizona it is highly likely you will buy into an area run by an HOA. You probably picture yourself getting the keys to your property and being able to come and go as you please without worrying about exterior upkeep and maintaining or increasing value within your area. This is the American dream— homeownership with limited responsibility and rising equity! Maybe —maybe not.

By writing this book we hope to bring you enough information to help you in your search when purchasing. We also wanted to provide information to those of you who are already in an HOA and need to better understand this form of government and your rights under this structured form of heaven or hell—and all that lies between!

Our wish is to inspire an elevation in the duties and obligations necessary for those taking on the huge responsibility of protecting investment and the "peaceful enjoyment" of ownership for others. Best summed up in one word: **fiduciary**.

SECTION II
WHERE DID HOAS COME FROM AND WHY?

———————⬩≫≪⬩———————

Nourish beginnings, let us nourish beginnings.
Not all things are blest, but the seeds of all
things are blest. The blessing is in the seed.

~ Muriel Rukeyser (1913-1980)
American Poet

———————⬩≫≪⬩———————

IN THE NINETEENTH century, the United States began to transform itself from a primarily agricultural society to an industrial one. A rapidly growing number of people took jobs in cities; however, most cities were overcrowded, dusty, and noisy and therefore, not a desirable location to call home. Commuter train rail lines made it possible for people to work within cities while living outside them and enjoy a better way of life! A series of "railroad communities" grew up along rail stations and were usually populated by middle-class families.

Thanks to the automobile, the twentieth century made people even more mobile, which led to a series of planned communities developed around the country. The houses tended to look essentially the same; however, in some communities several custom designs were built. These communities attracted more affluent families and there were few restrictions, but people who lived in them generally shared common ideas as to how streetscapes should look. Prior to Lyndon Johnson signing in the Fair Housing Law in 1968, homeowners associations as we know them today did not really exist... the associations similar to what we currently have existed in

5

early communities where people believed their purpose was to restrict residency based on race, religion or ethnic background.

LEVITTOWN: A NEW HOUSING CONCEPT [1]

> The first modern planned development was Levittown, built on the site of a potato field in Long Island, off the coast of New York. Builder William Levitt constructed a series of inexpensive but attractive homes that veterans could purchase with low-interest loans guaranteed by the federal government under the Servicemen's Readjustment Bill of 1944 (better known as the GI Bill). Between 1947 and 1951 more than 17,000 houses were built in and around the original Long Island community. Although Levittown residents were subject to restrictive covenants in their deeds, prohibiting such items as laundry lines in front yards, there was no formal homeowners association.

As suburban living continued to become a more attractive option, other similar developments were built—though on a smaller scale than Levittown. These developments were often more self-contained than large-scale communities, in that they maintained stricter standards regarding the appearance of the homes relative to both the structures and the landscaping. The general idea was that people who were looking for certain amenities and restrictions on

---

[1] FIND LAW:

http://realestate.findlaw.com/owning-a-home/history-of-homeowners-associations.html

pets or rules governing hedge planting, would be drawn to these communities; those who sought other amenities would look at other developments. Despite the logic behind this, it is not uncommon for residents of a Common Interest Development (CID) to find themselves in disagreement with their neighbors, or with the homeowners association, over seemingly minor infractions of the rules. What might be minor to some could be of great importance to others!

HOAs emerged in the mid-20th century, when increasing numbers of large-scale residential developments required more and more resources from cities and towns. There had to be a way to construct a plan that would allow great numbers of people to live in close proximity while still enjoying the right to own their own home without infringing on their neighbors or experiencing loss of freedom and privacy—yes, there had to be a better way!

> And so, HOAs were born and for the most part were successful in controlling large groups of people

In the beginning the HOAs governed horizontal housing and with the advent of popular subdivided vertical living HOAs took on a vast menu of new responsibilities.

The famous architect, Frank Lloyd Wright, in 1935 envisioned Broadacre City—an area that would be horizontal and made up of small, efficient affordable Usonian homes—where people would live, work and play. The city was never built, but his vision sparked a move to drive the popularity of such concepts as "Broadacre City: A New Community Plan."

Interestingly enough, the architect's ideal community was little more than a complete rejection of American homes of the entire first half of the 20th century. A prophetic vision of modern America, Broadacre-type cities, although a thought experience, dealt with Wright's belief cities could no longer be centralized, nor beholden to the pedestrian or the central business district.[2]

HOAs made it possible for members to enjoy common amenities at affordable prices without the hassle of maintenance. Cities loved HOAs—they brought in more taxes and less responsibility, particularly the ones in gated communities that took responsibility for their interior streets, etc. And, the cities removed themselves, as much as possible, from the problems and financial concerns occurring within the communities where problems became the concern of the HOA!

HOAs accomplished several benefits for the municipality. First, these amenities might have been burdened with property taxes, which would not be the case where amenities were owned by the municipality. Therefore, private amenities became owned by the HOA and taxed accordingly, which was beneficial to the cities.

The HOA is the cornerstone on which a planned residential or condominium community is built. It brings continuity and order to the community, it preserves the architectural integrity, and it maintains common elements. The association promotes the concept of "community" and protects the neighborhood's property values. Hopefully, and in a perfect world, this it true!

---

[2]   http://paleofuture.gizmodo.com/broadacre-city-frank-lloyd-wrights-unbuilt-suburban-ut-1509433082

MOST HOAS ARE SET-UP AS NON PROFIT CORPORATIONS — WHY?

AN HOA IS either a nonprofit corporation or unincorporated association, the purpose of which is to *manage a common interest real estate development*. An HOA is a form of government whose purpose is to govern the day-to-day management of the development; it is comprised of owners of property in the development, who elect members to a governing board to direct its activities. The boards of directors have designated powers and duties, and its directors also have individual duties.

An incorporated homeowners association is usually structured as a *non-profit mutual benefit* corporation and as such is exempt from certain governmental fees and taxes.

Usually the CC&R documents require the HOA to be incorporated since without incorporation, what would exist is a massive partnership, where each homeowner would be individually liable for anything the HOA would do. Incorporated associations are legally required to have directors. Arizona residents are guided and protected under Arizona Revised Statutes 10-1301 Non-Profit Corporation Act.

VARIABLES IN OWNERSHIP WITHIN A HOMEOWNER'S ASSOCIATION.

IN SOME STATES, the variable ownership, as found in Arizona, is broken down into Planned Community (Arizona Revised Statutes 33-1801 Planned Community Statutes) and Condominiums.

Revised Statutes 33-1201 Arizona Condominium Act.

THE PRINCIPAL DISTINCTION between Planned Community and Condominium HOAs involves the ownership of the common areas or *community* is a real estate development that is usually by a nonprofit corporation for the maintaining and improving the property. A ...ers to a real estate development in which certain ...ions are designated for separate ownership (units) and the unit owners designate the remainder for common ownership.[3] The main difference between condominiums, town homes and single-family homes is that there is no individual ownership of a plot of land. All of the land is owned in common by the homeowners. Even though a house, townhouse or apartment can actually be a condominium the only way to tell for sure is by checking the legal description.

> *Research your individual state for statutes relative to HOAs.*
> *http://www.hoa-usa.com/*

Ownership may consist of one of myriad formats: single family, townhouse, patio home and/or condominium. Each is discussed more fully in the following pages. Graphic images are included to provide a visual awareness as well.

---

[3] Arizona State Senate Issue Brief, November 25, Homeowners' Associations

http://www.azleg.gov/briefs/Senate/HOMEOWNERS'%20ASSOCIATIONS.pdf

―――――――∽∾∽――――――――

Single Family Homes

Single-family homes are detached properties on their own lot that do not share any walls with other properties. Single-family homes offer backyard space and more privacy. The HOA may be responsible for the care and regulation of community rules and maintenance of parks and community amenities/recreation areas.

―――――――∽∾∽――――――――

Townhouse

A **townhouse** is similar to a condo in that different individuals own each unit. However, townhouses can be multi-level units and are typically a row of similar units that share common walls on the left and/or right, *but not on the top/bottom*. Townhouses are similar to single-family homes in which you own the land that it sits on, but share at least one common wall. Townhouses also have an HOA that takes care of common areas/exteriors

11

Patio Homes

In **patio homes** you *also own the land* upon which your home sits, often in a suburban setting. Their neighborhood is usually made up of several houses that may be attached to each other, and may have shared walls between units or zero lot lines. Exterior maintenance and landscaping is almost always provided through an association and a fee is charged for this service.

Condominiums

Condominiums are real estate developments in which certain portions are designated for separate ownership (units) and the unit owners designate the remainder for common ownership. Each unit owner has an undivided percentage interest in the common elements, which are defined as all portions of a condominium, other than the units and they frequently include the land, exterior walls, walkways and recreational areas.

<u>*Mid-Rise Condominiums / Hi-Rise Condominiums*</u>

Mid-Rise: Approximately 4 to 10 stories high

Hi—Rise: A building that vertically rises seven or more stories

SECTION III
GOVERNING DOCUMENTS
FOR NON-PROFIT HOA

———— ⚬⚬ ————

The American Constitution is the greatest
governing document, and at some 7,000
words, just about the shortest.

~ Stephen Ambrose (1936-2002)
American Historian

———— ⚬⚬ ————

CC&R'S
(COVENANTS, CONDITIONS AND RESTRICTIONS)

CC&RS VARY WIDELY in content and length, but usually cover some of the following topics:

> they set the boundaries for the common area and for each unit or lot and present the legal description of the property;

> provide the allocation of the association operating costs among the owners; provide the mechanism for collecting owner payments as well as the allocation of owner voting rights;

> any restrictions on alienation of units and the rights and protection of mortgage lenders.

In Arizona:

"The governing documents create the legal foundation and organizational framework of an HOA. They consist of the Declaration of Covenants, Conditions and Restrictions (CC&Rs), the Articles of Incorporation, the Bylaws, and the Rules and Regulations. The CC&Rs constitute the enabling document, which is recorded with the county recorder and empowers the HOA to control

15

certain aspects of property use within the development, often including oversight and approval authority over the construction and alteration of homes.

> When a person buys a home in such a development, the person receives a copy of the CC&Rs and agrees to be bound by their terms. Thus, the CC&Rs form an enforceable contract between the HOA and the individual homeowner, thereby creating an Implied Covenant of Good Faith and Fair Dealing.

The Articles of Incorporation are required of incorporated HOAs and establish the HOA as a legal entity. They constitute the corporate charter and are filed with the Arizona Corporation Commission. The majority of HOAs formed since the mid-1980s are incorporated as nonprofit corporations and therefore have articles of incorporation. As such, incorporation as a non-profit provides greater statutory protection to the HOA board members, as well as to the unit or property owners, than remaining unincorporated. The *by-laws* set out the procedures for the internal governance and operation of the association. Each board member should know the sections of their state law that apply to HOAs. Board members must be familiar with the declaration or CC&Rs, the bylaws, and other controlling documents which form a contract among the homeowners within the HOA. The *declaration or covenants* (CC&R's) generally rule over conflicting provisions of the bylaws, and the *bylaws* generally govern over conflicting provisions of any rules and regulations or house rules adopted by the board. The CC&Rs may consist of the following sections:

1. Definitions

2. Submission of property

3. Description of the building units and the common elements

4. Association

5. Use of the common elements

6. Parking spaces

7. Common expenses

8. Mortgages

9. Insurance

10. Destruction

11. Condemnation

12. Obsolescence

13. Restoration or sale of property

14. Rights of owners in any distributions

15. Maintenance

16. Repairs and replacements

17. Right of access

18. Alterations

19. Additions or improvements

20. Decorating

21. Encroachments

22. Purchase of unit by Association

23. Use and occupancy restrictions

24. Architectural control

25. Party walls

26. Exemption of declarant from restrictions

27. Entry by Board or its agent

28. Roof leaks or repairs

29. Copy of Declaration to new members

30. Remedies

31. Amendment

32. Notices

33. Severability

34. Perpetuities and restraints on alienation

35. Rights and obligations

36. Performance or relief

37. Utility easements

38. First Mortgagee protection

39. Professional Management Agreement

40. Waive

> The phrase, use them or lose them, is sometimes directed toward the Board of Directors who may be "selective" and not consistent about enforcing all the CC&Rs, etc. They could be considered null and void by the courts if the Board routinely ignores Rules & Regs, CC&Rs, etc. or do not enforce the entire CC&Rs.

BY-LAWS

THE BYLAWS GOVERNS the way the HOA operates and contains the information needed to run it as a business. They cover such matters as:

How often the HOA holds meetings;

How the meetings are conducted; how many people are on the board; Membership voting rights; and the duties of the various offices of the *Board of Directors*, which include the following positions and descriptions of the general duties:

President

THE PRESIDENT SHALL be the chief executive officer of the corporation and shall preside at all meetings of the members and of the Board of Directors.[4] Shall have all of the general powers and duties, which are usually vested in the office of the President of a corporation, including, but not limited to, the *power to appoint committees* from among the members. The President is ultimately responsible to see that orders and resolutions of the Board of Directors are carried out. The President generally signs all contracts and other written instruments and co-signs all checks and promissory notes.

Qualifications to Consider When Choosing a President:

GOOD COMMUNICATOR; TEAM player: able to deal with the stress of angry homeowners without losing one's own cool. If it's an HOA that uses a manager; the President must be able to:

> set policy, make decisions and then step back and let the manager manage;

> not be a micromanager;

> answer all the questions or be willing to go to the proper sources for correct information;

> understand all the issues; have good "business sense," think rationally and think issues through to a logical conclusion.

> see the "big picture," and have a vision for how the community can improve;

> be a leader willing to stand up and lead with energy and enthusiasm and without self-interest, for the good of the community.

---

[4] Robert Rules of Order (http://www.rulesonline.com)

Vice-President

THE VICE-PRESIDENT will take the place of the President and perform duties whenever the President is absent or unable to act. If neither the President nor any Vice-President shall be able to act, the Board of Directors shall appoint some other member of the Board to do so on an interim basis. The Vice-President shall also perform such other duties as shall, from time to time, be imposed upon them by the Board of Directors, such as chairing a committee.

Treasurer

THE TREASURER RECEIVES and deposits in appropriate bank accounts all monies of the Association and disburses such funds as directed by resolution of the Board of Directors. The Treasurer signs all checks of the association; is keeper of the books of account; may cause an annual audit of the Association books to be made by a public accountant at the completion of each fiscal year; prepares an annual budget and a statement of income and expenditures to be presented to the membership in compliance with the civil code and delivers a copy of each to the members.

A management company would normally handle many of these duties but the Treasurer still has to oversee that they are being handled properly and in accordance with the Governing Documents and good business practices, such as requiring two signatures on all checks. Therefore, whether there is a management company involved, or not, the Treasurer has the overall responsibility to see that the Association funds are billed, collected, invested, accounted for and reported properly and accurately. The Treasurer does not have the sole authority to bind the Board or Association in agreements with third parties unless the Board specifically authorizes such actions.

Secretary

THE SECRETARY HAS the responsibility for keeping the minutes of all meetings of the Board of Directors and the members, and all necessary correspondence, the official minute book of the corporation, and as the Board of Directors shall from time to time designate such other duties. Hopefully, the Secretary will work to see that the minutes and information approved for dissemination are available to the membership.

Two Questions for the Board

1. What are their term limits?
2. Do they subscribe to a Code of Ethics?

ARTICLES OF INCORPORATION

THE ARTICLES ARE usually brief and contain only the basic information about the Association, its name, location, and its purpose.

Illustration: By examining two (2) different subdivisions we can stress the importance of electing the right Board of Directors and choosing the right property management team:

Patio Home

1. 185 units with square footage from 1500 to 1925.
2. In the last six months the average selling price is $404,500.00.
3. The monthly maintenance fee is $250.00.

This means the total aggregate dollar value of the subdivision is $74,832,500.00 and the total annual maintenance fees collected are $555,000.00. When you think of a subdivision in terms of monetary value, it makes you aware that the running of an association is a very big deal. What would you expect in terms of management for a

21

multi-million dollar property? What would be your concerns for caring for the property, maintaining or increasing value and protecting the half a million dollars in collected fees?

Mid-rise condominium:

1. 185 units with square footage ranging from 850 to 2150.

2. In the last six months the average selling price is $126,500

3. The monthly average maintenance fee is $221.00.

This indicates the total aggregate dollar value of the subdivision is $23,402.500.00 and the total annual maintenance fees collected are $490,620.00

Again, this is a multimillion-dollar property with close to a half a million dollars in revenue collected each year. Your concerns would be the same as above, adding to the equation for concerns for maintaining elevators, A/C, roofs, halls etc. Structural concerns would be paramount and would require special knowledge and procedures to manage the building (s).

In both cases, hiring the "right" management and electing the "right" board members would be key to running a successful HOA.

SECTION IV

RESPONSIBILITIES OF T...

―――――※―――――

It is our responsibilities, not ourselv...
should take seriously.

~ Peter Ustinov (1921-2004)
English Actor

―――――※―――――

OPERATING A HOMEOWNERS association carries with it many of the very same duties and responsibilities as overseeing any other business. Serving as a board member can be a valuable and rewarding experience that should be undertaken by those who see it as an opportunity to serve their fellow neighbors while protecting and enhancing the assets of the community.

The Governing Body (or **Board of Directors**) of the HOA is responsible for the management of all aspects of the Association and is responsible to preserve architectural integrity and maintain the common elements and promote the concept of "community" and protect the neighborhood's property values; It may delegate management of certain activities to other persons or businesses, such as a property management service, but it must retain fiduciary responsibility and ultimate control.

> The classic vision of an HOA is to protect, maintain and enhance the value of the community.

WHAT ARE THE DUTIES OF A BOARD OF DIRECTORS?

UPON THE ELECTION to the board, Directors become fiduciaries with powers to act on behalf of the Association. As fiduciaries, Directors are held to a higher standard of conduct and have two primary duties:

duty of care—must be diligent and careful in preforming the duties they have undertaken;

duty of loyalty—must act in the best interest of the association even if at the expense of their own interest and they must always be accountable to their membership; transparency is a must!

FIDUCIARY DUTY AND THE BUSINESS JUDGMENT RULE

THE BOARD MEMBERS owe a *Fiduciary Duty* (A duty to act for someone else's benefit, while subordinating one's personal interest to that of the other person.) According to *Black's Law Dictionary*, it is the highest standard of duty implied by law (e.g., trustee, guardian) to the homeowners to manage and operate the Association using the care that an ordinarily prudent person would use under the same or similar circumstances (The Business Judgment Rule). This means that the Board must exercise business judgment in making decisions while operating or managing the association. Business judgment involves making rational, informed decisions in good faith. The board must:

Strictly follow the law and its Governing Documents and apply and enforce them in a fair and uniform manner.

Obtain and consider all of the relevant facts and circumstances, identify the various options available to the board, and carefully weigh which course of action would be in the best interests of the association and its membership as a whole.

Board members cannot act out of passion or prejudice, personal self-interest or gain, or through revenge or other negative motivations. The rational basis for all decisions must be the best interests of the association consistent with its purposes.

SECTION V
BOARD OF DIRECTORS:
RESPONSIBILITY
BUILDING A SENSE OF COMMUNITY

*Law; an ordinance of reason for the
common good, made by him who has care of
the community.*

~ Thomas Aquinas (1225-1274)
Italian theologian.

WHAT ARE SOME of the ways the Board of Directors can implement their responsibility for preserving architectural integrity, maintain the common elements, promote the concept of "community" and protect the neighborhood property values? The following tools, as such, are the answer to connect and communicate at the highest level possible to promote connectivity within a greater community… a community with a deep commonality—structured and fairly regulated home ownership—under the umbrella of and HOA.

Website

DEVELOPING A WEBSITE as per HOA Sites[5] that can help reduce printing, mailing and administrative costs and provide residents 24/7 access to their neighborhood information while promoting the

---

[5] HOA Website: http://www.hoa-sites.com

neighborhood's property and communicating effectively with residents by posting:

1. Announcements;

2. Various documents such as CC&R's, HOA rules, etc.;

3. Photo albums and message boards;

4. Events calendar;

5. Homes for sale;

6. Surveys and/or Reserve Study;

7. Community directories;

8. Reviews/homeowners communication;

9. Meeting minutes for residents and Board review;

10. Generate Revenue: selling classified ads, banner ads, bulletins and announcement.

PLANNED COMMUNITY

ANY PLANNED COMMUNITY or condominium that has more than 50 or more residences may want to consider hiring a State licensed *Property Management Company* that requires overall supervision by the Designated Broker and whose managers have, in addition, a Certified Manager of Community Associations (CMCA) certification credentials.

> **Unless the Community Management is licensed** there can be a real problem with accountability. Since there is no requirement for licensed HOA managers in Arizona, there is nowhere to go other than an attorney, the police or attorney general's office when abuse of financial responsibility is suspected.

Typical Duties of a Property Manager

According to IREM (Institute of Real Estate Management):[6]

1. **Communication:** Maintain communication with the board, association members/owners and vendors; Respond to letters and log calls from owners. Send notices of annual meetings

2. **Fiscal Management:** Collect assessments; insure bills are paid; Produce financial Statements; establish a draft budget for the board and implement budget policy; insure tax forms are completed and taxes are paid, as appropriate.

3. **Advice and Consultation:** Advise the board on governing documents; Refer the board to other professional advisors (e.g. attorneys, CPAs, engineers); Research insurance coverage and process claims

4. **Record Keeping:** Maintain files for each member of the association/owner. Maintain records for the association; process initial Architectural Control Committee (ACC) applications

5. **Property Management and Maintenance:** Interview, hire, supervise and terminate association employees, when necessary; Negotiate contracts—with board approval. Monitor contract vendors such as landscapers and custodial services; Inspect and maintain comment elements and handle emergency situations.

If licensed, the actions of the managers would be covered by the rules and supervision of the real estate department. The department exists for the protection of the public and also provides a recovery fund[7] (A.R.S 32-2186) for the victims of wrongdoing. In order to be licensed you must go through an extensive licensing curriculum to meet the requirements for each of the positions listed as follows.[8]

---

[6] Property Management:
https://www.irem.org/education/learningtoolbox/homeownersassoc

[7] Real Estate Recovery Fund: A.R.S. 32-2186
http://www.azleg.gov/ars/32/02186.htm

[8] ADRE Licensing:
http://www.azre.gov/Lic/Documents/Original_Licensing_Brochure_2_2015.pdf

Note: Our school does not offer licensing education, but there are several that do.

Arizona Salesperson's License:

COMPLETE 90 HOURS of classroom education through an ADRE approved school, pass the school final exam; register for and pass the State Exam and take at least 24 hours or renewal classes every 2 years.

Qualifications for an Arizona Broker's License:

PROVIDE PROOF OF 3 years actual full-time experience as a salesperson; complete 90 hours of in classroom pre-licensing education through an ADRE approved school, pass the school final examination, and register for and pass the State Exam. In order to keep your license active you must go through license renewal regularly. Associate brokers must complete 24 hours renewal courses every 2 years and a self-employed Broker or a Designated Broker must complete 30 hours renewal courses every 2 years.

BOOK OF GOVERNING

PROVIDING A BOOK of Governing to each board member and Committee Chairman is most helpful, and the contents frequently consist of:

1. General administrative issues such as Board and committee duties and responsibilities,
2. Yearly calendar and activities;
3. Board policy resolutions (updated periodically);
4. Logs—such as Architectural control change requests;
5. Hearings;
6. Tenants;
7. Pet registrations;

8. Violations of CC&R's:

9. Financial;

10. Monthly financial statements;

11. Reserve analysis and status;

12. Meeting minutes;

13. Meetings and Annual meetings:

14. Legal issues;

15. Board promulgated rules and regulations;

16. CC&R's and By-Laws and Code of Ethics statement.

17. Minutes of all board and owner meetings;

18. Insurance policies;

19. Contracts;

20. Leases, and other agreements in effect;

21. Current list of the names and addresses of the members;

22. Copies of ballots and proxies from past elections;

23. Itemized accounting of the budgeted and actual receipts and expenditures of the HOA with supporting budgetary (Reserve Study) and financial documents.

24. An explanation of the Federal Fair Housing Law and the state Fair Housing Law and their importance in running the association in an inclusive manner without violating these most important laws.

ESTABLISH COMMITTEES

Architectural Control

THE ARCHITECTURAL COMMITTEE is responsible for maintaining the aesthetic and structural integrity of the association and enforcing the *CC&Rs*. They review applications for modifications, additions, or architectural changes in the community. It is also their duty to stay informed on environmental issues that could affect the homeowners desire to upgrade their homes. Favoritism for one neighbor over another cannot come into play when approving applications for improvements.

Landscaping

MAINTAINS AND IMPROVES, when needed, the grass, trees, plants, flowers, and grounds located in the common properties. Makes recommendations for flower and tree plantings or other landscaping improvements to the common areas and oversee the seasonal maintenance activities. Water issues are important and often addressed by the city and state, which frequently reach out to HOAs in an effort to help them.

Financial

THE ROLE OF the Finance Committee is primarily to provide financial oversight that includes budgeting and financial planning, financial reporting, and the creation and monitoring of internal controls and accountability policies. This committee can be instrumental in promoting proper audits on a regular basis.

Website

DEVELOP AND MAINTAIN the website, the Association Directory, handbook, newsletters, updates and all pertinent neighborhood information on the website

Safety and Security

TO ASSIST IN improving, establishing and enforcing community security and emergency and other safety standards:

RESERVE STUDY
AND/OR
A RESERVE STUDY SUMMARY

THE RESERVE STUDY Summary lists all major components/assets, their useful life, and their Remaining Useful Life. These will be shown in columns for every major component. A quick glance at the Remaining Useful Life Column provides a feel for the health of the Association. If you see items with Remaining Useful Live at *zero* that simply means the item should have been replaced, but wasn't. Most reserve studies do not go into negative status, such as a negative (-) 5 years, to let you know the item should have been replaced five years ago. Most often they will just reflect "Ø".

A Reserve Study is a long-term capital budget planning tool that identifies the current status of the Reserve Fund and a stable and equitable funding plan to offset on-going potential deterioration, which may result in insufficient funds when those anticipated major common area expenditures actually occur. The Reserve Study consists of two parts: the physical analysis and the financial analysis—documents that are often prepared by an outside independent consultant for the benefit of the administrators (Board of Directors) of a property having multiple owners, such as a condominium association or homeowners association. It contains an assessment of the state of the commonly owned property components as determined by the particular association's CC&Rs and bylaws. Reserve Studies however are not limited only to condominiums and can be created for other properties such as resort (shared vacation ownership) properties, apartment buildings, worship facilities, private schools, private golf/social clubs, and office parks.

Reserve Studies are in essence planning tools designed to help the board anticipate, and prepare for, the property's major repair and replacement projects. For example, such projects would include:

replacement of the roof on the building(s), replacement of the boiler, retrofit of the fire alarm devices, and resurfacing of the roadways.

Maintaining a reserve fund not only meets legal, fiduciary and professional requirements—it can also minimize the need for special assessments and could also enhance resale values.[9]

The Board of Directors must make decisions about the funding goals of the association and should consult with the association's own attorney, accountant, or other advisors, as necessary.

Because the board has a fiduciary duty to manage association funds and property, a replacement reserve budget is very important.[10]

Physical Analysis for Consultants

1. Quantification of components.
2. Documentation of maintenance assumptions and recommendations.
3. Identification of useful life and remaining life of components, and replacement year.
4. Estimation of replacement cost in current and future dollars.

Funding Analysis for Consultants

1. Spreadsheet modeling of reserve funding, and development of solution(s) meeting the funding goals of the association.
2. Calculation of cash balance of reserve account by year.
3. Estimation and explanation of reserve deficit.
4. Recommendation of needed increases in reserve portion of assessment.

---

[9] Wikipedia: https://en.wikipedia.org/wiki/Reserve_study

[10] State of California, Dept. of Real Estate, Reserve Study Guidelines for HOAs
http://www.dre.ca.gov/files/pdf/re25.pdf

5. Recommendation of needed special assessments and timing of assessments.

6. Preparation of statement of limitations and assumptions of reserve analysis.

7. Preparation of reserve study information for the proforma-operating budget.

Once the work tasks have been determined, the Board must select the consultants or contractors, if any, who will perform all or part of the work. In turn, consideration should be given in hiring an independent engineering, appraisal, or construction cost-estimating firm to perform the Physical Analysis and hiring an independent accountant experienced with community associations to produce the Funding Analysis and pro-forma operating budget. This can be accomplished by hiring the current management company, or another qualified entity, to perform both studies and incorporate the results into the pro-forma operating budget.

The Importance of Reserves

Boards often neglect the issue of reserves. It is not enough to budget existing costs and expenses, but they must establish a reserve for two main purposes.

Emergencies: Unless the board has a fund from which to handle emergency or unexpected costs, the Association will be vulnerable. The Board must assume that some unexpected expenditures will be necessary.

Deferred Repair or Replacement: The Board must find out the estimated useful life of its structural and mechanical components, surfaces of the buildings and common areas, energy systems and equipment. They then can determine a reasonable amount for the owners' monthly contributions to a reserve. Unless this reserve is established, the homeowners who use the property will not be contributing towards the replacement of the property in the future, leaving future owners with the full cost of major repair or restoration (such as roofing, paving, siding, HVAC, and other major components).

Reserve Red Flags:

1. The HOA has no established list of major components; there is no policy to distinguish reserve expenditures from operating expenses.

2. There is no clear funding goal stated.

3. A physical analysis has not been conducted

4. A funding analysis has not been conducted

5. Information on remaining life and current replacement cost has not been prepared for all major components

6. The *pro-forma* operating budget does not contain reserve study information or assumptions

7. The HOA does not have a documented maintenance schedule and related assumptions for each major component and there are no separate bank account(s) for reserve funds.

RULES AND REGULATIONS

RULES AND REGULATIONS often address specific matters related to the use of the property that are not specifically covered by the CC&Rs. This needs to be looked at carefully. They may cover the following;

1. Animals and pets;

2. Motor vehicles;

3. Visitor parking;

4. Towing;

5. Trash containers;

6. Signs;

7. Use of swimming pool and spa;

8. Use of fitness room;

9. Front doors;

10. Patio and balconies;

11. Satellite dishes;

12. Window coverings;

13. Penetration of floors or walls;

14. Rental of units;

15. Bicycle storage;

16. Penalties;

17. Reporting violations, etc.

Dispute Process

a) Effective July 1, 2016 Arizona Department of Real Estate began handling the Homeowners Association (HOA) Dispute Process *(see SB1530, 32-2199 thru 2199.05) or www.azre.gov for details)* but does not limit the legal rights of the parties to further pursue matters, or consider.

b) Alternative Dispute Resolution (ADR) according to CAI (Community Association Institute).[11]

c) ADR is less costly and can be more productive than litigation. It is comprised of three phases: negotiation, mediation, and arbitration. In negotiation, the parties identify the issues, educate one another about their needs and interests, propose settlement options, and bargain over the final resolution. In mediation, a neutral mediator facilitates the negotiation between and Associations and residents to help them agree on a solution that is acceptable to each of them. In arbitration, a neutral arbitrator hears both sides of the case and renders a decision based on evidence and testimony. An arbitrator's decision is a legal and can be as binding, if agreed upon, a s a court decision.

---

[11] Community Association Institute (CAI), Best practices, page 18

http://www.cairf.org/publications/best_practices.aspx

STRATEGIC PLANNING

ESTABLISH A SET of priorities; achievable; measurable and time sensitive; flexible and responsive to changing conditions; short and simple; a unit, not a menu; the means to an end in itself and based on a three to five-year period; energy efficiency "Building Green."

FINANCIAL REPORT(S)

1. **Audit:** An examination of an organization's accounting records and procedures by an independent certified public accountant for the purpose of verifying the fairness of the presentation of financial statements. Financial experts recommend that a CPA familiar with community associations perform an audit annually, minimally every other year.

2. **Review:** It is less thorough than an audit; it provides some assurance that the financial statements are consistent with typical trends without the detailed examination obtained in an audit.

3. **Compilation**: Is a presentation of financial statements prepared by an accountant, but does not provide any level of assurance regarding the financial statements.

* See again footnote #9

FANNIE MAE/FREDDIE MAC/FHA APPROVAL

SOME ISSUES ARE best handled by the professional with the greatest expertise. With this in mind, we invited Kelly Zitlow, VP, Cherry Creek Mortgage, to share with you information about condo's from a lending assessment.

FROM A HOME lending perspective, condo's undergo a more extensive property analysis than that of a single family residence. If a buyer is using a home loan when purchasing or refinancing a condo the lender will not only evaluate the borrower's qualifications but also evaluate the property as well as the condominium project in entirety.

To perform this review the lender will require a Condo Questionnaire be completed by the HOA. Once completed the lender will review and determine if the condominium project meets the lending guidelines. Guidelines vary by loan type but in general, the lender is using the information from the Condo questionnaire to assess the stability and financial strength of the condo project. New build project guidelines differ from established communities. Below are some of the specifics lenders are focused on when evaluating a condo project:

Percentage of owner occupied, second home and investment property.

Budget must have a certain percentage of the total budget allocated to replacement reserves.

Percentage of home owner's that are delinquent in paying their HOA dues.

If a single person or entity own more than a certain percentage of the units.

If the total square footage of the project can be used for non-residential purposes.

Ineligible projects may include those with timeshare units, condo hotels, multiple units under a single deed or mortgage and projects that are currently in litigation.

Insurance must meet minimum requirements.

Condo's can offer a low maintenance lifestyle and which interests many buyers. It's important to be sure buyers utilizing financing understand the lender's process in evaluating the condo project when underwriting the home loan as it can impact their ability to obtain financing.

Kelly Zitlow, VP,
Cherry Creek Mortgage,
kzitlow@ccmclending.com
http://www.kellyzitlow.com/

The Board has the responsibility to stay on top of issues that affect the salability or value of the units that may require a project to be warrantable before Lenders can provide financing to facilitate a new loan or obtain a Reverse Mortgage.

MEETINGS

ALTHOUGH IT WOULD be desirable for each member of the community to attend meetings, it is not always possible.

Owners deserve to be kept in the loop. Whether they live in another state, another country or have conflicts that prevent them from going to the meetings, they deserve to be updated and included in all matters pertaining to their property.

For reasons of health, time constraints or a million other reasons a homeowner may elect to not attend meetings and that is their right. Their reasons are personal and are not the business of the board, yet they can still add value and should be consulted and informed.

> The workings of the HOA need to be disseminated to all and not kept in secret for a "privileged" few. The HOA is not a private club; it must be transparent and inclusive!

HOAs and All That Jazz
Burton and Susan Sweetow

In this day of technology, boards must move forward to embrace the advantages of new ways to be proactive in reaching out to their neighbors. Through proper communication with the owners, physical presence at meetings might not be necessary. Through use of websites, email and even Skyping... an active membership could thrive!

HOAs IN THE NEWS

You have to have really wide reading habits and pay attention to the news and just everything that's going on in the world: you need to. If you get this right, then the writing is a piece of cake.

~ Terry Pratchett (1948-2015)
English author.

THERE IS NOTHING quite like a good lawsuit to send a "red-flag" message that people need to be aware of what goes on in the workings of HOAs. The following stories are real; they happened within the State of Arizona over the past several years—many most likely had some impact on any modifications made in the Statutes, or within the management of HOA's to ensure adequate homeowner protection.

The headlines posted by Jason Barry on CBS5 Arizona News on November 21, 2012 was such that many people immediately were interested in the story headline that followed: **Lawsuit filed against HOA management companies.** The story broke about HOA management companies in the San Tan Valley area of the Phoenix Metro Valley who were accused of "charging illegal collection and filing fees."

The class-action lawsuit, filed in Maricopa County Superior Court, was based on violations of the Fair Debt Collection Practices Act. The suit came about when a local couple went to CBS5, claiming their HOA management company had not only charged them hundreds of dollars in unnecessary fees, but also put a lien on their home. There was some confusion as to their quarterly fees and other assessments, which "ballooned" what the couple owed—to a management firm who was not amenable to working things out with the homeowners.

What came out of the suit was awareness that thousands of additional homeowners in the Valley shared similar experiences. The attorney filing the lawsuit indicated many of the two dozen HOA management companies named in the suit were doing pretty much what they wanted, feeling "there's no one looking over their shoulder."

The primary management firm asserted the claims had no merit and were confident the practices would be vindicated. However, after taking the case to the Supreme Court, at the very end of a lengthy 11-page Advisory Opinion, the following conclusion was provided.

> *Many homeowner and condominium associations have turned to professional community association management companies to help them fulfill their day-to-day duties in an efficient and cost-effective manner. This opinion provides guidance on the scope and extent of legal services (UPL Advisory Op. 12-01 p. 11) that these professional community management companies are permitted to provide. Except under the limited circumstances outlined above, community association management company personnel would be engaging in the unauthorized practice of law by drafting documents for and providing legal services to homeowner and condominium associations under Rule 31, Ariz. R. Sup. Ct., and Arizona Code of Judicial Administration § 7-208*

The previous issue was not an isolated incident! In June 2016, a rather upset homeowner contacted ABC15, to discuss the strong-arm tactics of her HOA. The homeowner was fully in compliance with the terms of her CC&Rs; however the Board was using a harsh and heavy-handed tactic in an attempt to force compliance to rulings that didn't exist. After being contacted by ABC15, the management further investigated and found the homeowner was, indeed, fully in compliance with the rulings.

HOAs and All That Jazz
Burton and Susan Sweetow

From politics to embezzlement...

from neighbors at war to grassroots groups seeking to change legislation...

you need to be aware, regardless the position you are in as a homeowner, in a management position, or as a board member or legal representative. If you want to be more aware of what is reported in the news relative to HOAs, you may want to bookmark the link for *About HOAs*—an organization-based site providing consumer information, resources and news.

http://www.abouthoas.org/?cat=19

SECTION VI
ARIZONA CONDOMINIUM ACT

---

*Therefore, a person should first be changed by
a teacher's instructions, and guided by
principles of ritual.
Only then can he observe the rules of courtesy
and humility, obey the conventions and rules
of society, and achieve order.*

~ Xun Kuang (310 BC-237 BC)
Chinese Philosopher

IN PRESENTING THE rulings that bind HOAs, the best—and only valid—information comes from the Arizona Statutes. In order to keep this book as evergreen as possible, some of the information you will find in the following pages are merely lists, which reflect the nature of information in the laws governing the State of Arizona, relative to HOAs.

ARTICLE 1
GENERAL PROVISIONS

§ 33-1201 Applicability

§ 33-1202 Definitions

§ 33-1203 Variation

§ 33-1204 Separate titles and taxation

§ 33-1205 Applicability of local ordinances, rules and building codes

§ 33-1206 Eminent domain

§ 33-1207 Severability

ARTICLE 2
CREATION, ALTERATION AND
TERMINATION OF CONDOMINIUMS

§ 33-1211 Creation of condominium

§ 33-1212 Unit boundaries

§ 33-1213 Construction and validity of declaration and bylaw

§ 33-1214 Description of units

§ 33-1215 Contents of declaration

§ 33-1216 Leasehold condominiums

§ 33-1217 Allocation of common element interests, votes and common expense liabilities.

§ 33-1218 Limited common elements

§ 33-1219 Plat

§ 33-1220 Exercise of development rights

§ 33-1221 Alterations of units

§ 33-1222 Relocation of boundaries between adjoining units

§ 33-1223 Subdivision of units

§ 33-1224 Easement for encroachments

§ 33-1225 Use for sale purposes

§ 33-1226 Easement to facilitate exercise of special declarant rights

§ 33-1227 Amendment of declaration

§ 33-1228 Termination of condominium

§ 33-1229 Rights of secured lenders

§ 33-1230 Merger or consolidation of Condominiums

ARTICLE 3
MANAGEMENT OF THE CONDOMINIUM

§ 33-1241 Organization of unit owners' association

§ 33-1242 Powers of unit owners' association; notice to unit owner of violation

§ 33-1243 Board of Directors and Officers; conflict, power, limitations; removal; annual audit; applicability

§ 33-1244 Transfer of special declarant rights

§ 33-1245 Termination of contracts and leases of Declarant applicability

§ 33-1246 Bylaws

§ 33-1247 Upkeep of the condominium

§ 33-1248 Open meetings; exceptions

§ 33-1249 Quorums; applicability

§ 33-1250 Voting; proxies; absentee ballots; applicability; definition

§ 33-1251 Tort and contract liability

§ 33-1252 Conveyance or encumbrance of common elements

§ 33-1252.01 Conveyance of certain real property

§ 33-1253 Insurance

§ 33-1254 Surplus monies

§ 33-1255 Assessments for common expenses; applicability

§ 33-1256 Lien for assessments; priority; mechanics' and materialmen's liens; applicability

§ 33-1257 Other liens affecting the condominium

§ 33-1258 Association financial and other records; applicability

§ 33-1259 Association as trustee

§ 33-1260 Resale of units; information required; fees; civil penalty; applicability; definition

§ 33-1260.01 Rental property; unit owner and agent information fee; disclosure

§ 33-1261 Flag display; for sale, rent or lease signs; political signs and activities; applicability

§ 33-1270 Department of real estate; enforcement

ARTICLE 4
ADMINISTRATION OF THE CONDOMINIUM ACT

33-1201. Applicability

This chapter applies to all condominiums created within this state without regard to the date the condominium was created.

3-1202. Definitions

In the condominium documents, unless specifically provided otherwise or the context otherwise requires, and in this chapter:

1. "Affiliate of a declarant" means any person who controls, is controlled by or is under common control with a declarant.

2. "Allocated interests" means the undivided interests in the common elements, the common expense liability and votes in the association allocated to each unit.

3. "Articles of incorporation" means the instrument by which an incorporated association or unit owners' association is formed and organized under this state's corporate statutes.

4. "Association" or "unit owners' association" means the unit owners' association organized under section 33-1241.

5. "Board of directors" means the body, regardless of its name, designated in the declaration and given general management powers to act on behalf of the association.

6. "Bylaws" means the bylaws required by section 33-1246.

7. "Common elements" means all portions of a condominium other than the units.

8. "Common expense liability" means the liability for common expenses allocated to each unit pursuant to section 33-1217.

9. "Common expenses" means expenditures made by or financial liabilities of the association, together with any allocations to reserves.

10. "Condominium" means real estate, portions of which are designated for separate ownership and the remainder of which is designated for common ownership solely by the owners of the separate portions. Real estate is not a condominium unless the undivided interests in the common elements are vested in the unit owners.

11. "Condominium documents" means the declaration, bylaws, articles of incorporation, if any, and rules, if any.

12. "Declarant" means any person or group of persons who reserves, is granted or succeeds to any special declarant right.

13. "Declaration" means any instruments, however denominated, that create a condominium and any amendments to those instruments.

14. "Development rights" means any right or combination of rights reserved by or granted to a declarant in the declaration to do any of the following:

    a) Add real estate to a condominium.

    b) Create easements, units, common elements or limited common elements within a condominium.

    c) Subdivide units, convert units into common elements or convert common elements into units.

    d) Withdraw real estate from a condominium.

    e) Make the condominium part of a larger condominium or planned community.

    f) Amend the declaration during any period of declarant control, pursuant to section 33-1243, subsection E, to comply with applicable law or to correct any error or inconsistency in the declaration, if the amendment does not adversely affect the rights of any unit owner.

g) Amend the declaration during any period of declarant control, pursuant to section 33-1243, subsection E, to comply with the rules or guidelines, in effect from time to time, of any governmental or quasi-governmental entity or federal corporation guaranteeing or insuring mortgage loans or governing transactions involving mortgage instruments.

15. "Identifying number" means a symbol or address that identifies one unit in a condominium.

16. "Leasehold condominium" means a condominium in which all or a portion of the real estate is subject to a lease the expiration or termination of which will terminate the condominium or reduce its size.

17. "Limited common element" means a portion of the common elements specifically designated as a limited common element in the declaration and allocated by the declaration or by operation of section 33-1212, paragraph 2 or 4 for the exclusive use of one or more but fewer than all of the units.

18. "Person" means a natural person, corporation, business trust, estate, trust, partnership, association, joint venture, government, governmental subdivision or agency, or other legal or commercial entity. In the case of a subdivision trust, as defined in section 6-801, person means the beneficiary of the trust who holds the right to subdivide, develop or sell the real estate rather than the trust or trustee.

19. "Real estate" means any legal, equitable, leasehold or other estate or interest in, over or under land, including structures, fixtures and other improvements and interests which by custom, usage or law pass with a conveyance of land though not described in the contract of sale or instrument of conveyance. Real estate includes parcels with or without upper or lower boundaries and spaces that may be filled with air or water.

20. "Rules" means the provisions, if any, adopted pursuant to the declaration or bylaws governing maintenance and use of the units and common elements.

21. "Special declarant rights" means any right or combination of rights reserved by or granted to a declarant in the declaration to do any of the following:

    a) Construct improvements provided for in the declaration.

    b) Exercise any development right.

    c) Maintain sales offices, management offices, signs advertising the condominium, and models.

    d) Use easements through the common elements for the purpose of making improvements within the condominium or within real estate, which may be added to the condominium.

    e) Appoint or remove any officer of the association or any board member during any period of declarant control.

22. "Unit" means a portion of the condominium designated for separate ownership or occupancy.

23. "Unit owner" means a declarant or other person who owns a unit or, unless otherwise provided in the lease, a lessee of a unit in a leasehold condominium whose lease expires simultaneously with any lease the expiration or termination of which will remove the unit from the condominium but does not include a person having an interest in a unit solely as security for an obligation. In the case of a contract for conveyance, as defined in section 33-741, of real property, unit owner means the purchaser of the unit.

33-1203. Variations

Except as expressly provided in this chapter, the provisions of this chapter shall not be varied by agreement and rights conferred by this chapter shall not be waived. A person shall not use any device to evade the limitations or prohibitions of this chapter.

33-1204. Separate titles and taxation

A. If there is a unit owner other than a declarant, each unit that has been created, together with its interest in the common elements, constitutes for all purposes a separate parcel of real estate.

B. Except as provided in subsection C, if there is a unit owner other than a declarant, each unit shall be separately taxed and assessed, and no separate tax or assessment may be rendered against any common elements.

C. Any portion of the common elements which the declarant reserves the right to withdraw from the condominium shall be separately taxed and assessed against the declarant and the declarant alone is liable for payment of those taxes, as long as the declarant retains this right to withdraw.

D. If there is no unit owner other than a declarant, the real estate comprising the condominium shall be taxed and assessed as a single parcel.

33-1205. Applicability of local ordinances, rules and building codes

A. A zoning, subdivision or building code or other real estate use law, ordinance or rule shall not prohibit a condominium form of ownership or impose any requirement on a condominium which it would not impose on a physically identical development under a different form of ownership.

B. Except as provided in subsection A, this chapter does not invalidate or modify any provision of any zoning, subdivision or building code or other real estate use law, ordinance or rule.

33-1206. Eminent domain

A. If a unit is acquired by eminent domain, or if part of a unit is acquired by eminent domain leaving the unit owner with a remnant which may not practically or lawfully be used for any purpose permitted by the declaration, the award must compensate the unit owner for his unit and its interest in the common elements, regardless of whether any common elements are acquired. On acquisition, unless the decree otherwise provides, that unit's allocated interests are automatically reallocated to the remaining units in proportion to the respective allocated interests of those units before the taking, and the association shall promptly prepare, execute and record an amendment to the declaration reflecting the reallocations. Any remnant of a unit remaining after part of a unit is taken under this subsection becomes a common element.

B. Except as provided in subsection A of this section, if part of a unit is acquired by eminent domain the award must compensate the unit owner for the reduction in value of the unit and its interest in the common elements, regardless of whether any common elements are acquired. On acquisition, unless the decree otherwise provides, all of the following apply:

1. The unit's allocated interests are reduced in proportion to the reduction in the size of the unit or on any other basis specified in the declaration.

2. The portion of the allocated interests divested from the partially acquired unit is automatically reallocated to that unit and the remaining units in proportion to the respective allocated interests of those units before the taking, with the partially acquired unit participating in the reallocation on the basis of its reduced allocated interests.

C. If part of the common elements is acquired by eminent domain, the portion of the award attributable to the common elements taken shall be paid to the association for the benefit of the unit owners. Unless the declaration provides otherwise, any portion of the award attributable to the acquisition of a limited common element shall be equally divided among the owners of the units to which that limited common element was allocated at the time of acquisition.

D. The court decree shall be recorded in every county in which any portion of the condominium is located.

E. If all of the units of the condominium are acquired by eminent domain, the condominium is terminated and the provisions of section 33-1228 apply.

F. This section does not restrict the rights of lessees, mortgagees, declarants or any other person holding an interest in a unit or its common elements from receiving separate compensation or a portion of the compensation payable, or both, pursuant to this section.

33-1207. Severability

If any provision of this chapter or its application to any person or circumstances is held invalid, the invalidity does not affect other provisions or applications of the chapter which can be given effect without the invalid provisions or application, and to this end the provisions of this chapter are severable.

33-1211. Creation of Condominium

A condominium may only be created pursuant to this chapter by recording a declaration in the same manner as a deed in each county in which any portion of the condominium is located. The declaration shall be indexed in the name of the condominium, the name of the association and otherwise as required by law.

33-1212. Unit Boundaries

Except as provided by the declaration:

1. If walls, floors or ceilings are designated as boundaries of a unit, all lath, furring, wallboard, plasterboard, plaster, paneling, tiles, wallpaper, paint, finished flooring and any other materials constituting any part of the finished surfaces are a part of the unit, and all other portions of the walls, floors or ceilings are a part of the common elements.

2. If any chute, flue, duct, wire, conduit, bearing wall, bearing column or other fixture lies partially within and partially outside the designated boundaries of a unit, any portion serving only that unit is a limited common element allocated solely to that unit and any portion serving more than one unit or any portion of the common elements is a part of the common elements.

3. Subject to the provisions of paragraph 2, all spaces, interior partitions and other fixtures and improvements within the boundaries of a unit are a part of the unit.

4. Any shutters, awnings, window boxes, doorsteps, stoops, porches, balconies, entryways or patios, and all exterior doors and windows or other fixtures designed to serve a single unit, but located outside the unit's boundaries, are limited common elements allocated exclusively to that unit.

33-1213. Construction and Validity of Declaration and Bylaws

A. All provisions of the condominium documents are severable.

B. The rule against perpetuities shall not be applied to defeat any provision of the condominium documents.

C. Except to the extent inconsistent with this chapter:

1. If a conflict exists between the provisions of the declaration and the other condominium documents, the declaration prevails.

2. If a conflict exists between the provisions of the articles of incorporation and the bylaws or rules, the articles of incorporation prevail.

3. If a conflict exists between the provisions of the bylaws and the rules, the bylaws prevail.

D. Title to a unit and common elements is not rendered unmarketable or otherwise affected by reason of an insubstantial failure of any condominium documents to comply with this chapter.

33-1214. Description of Units

A description of a unit which sets forth the name of the condominium, the recording data for the declaration, the county or counties in which the condominium is located and the identifying number of the unit is a sufficient legal description of that unit and all common elements, rights, obligations and interests appurtenant to that unit.

33-1215. Contents of Declaration

A. The declaration shall contain:

1. The name of the condominium, which shall include the word "condominium" or be followed by the words "a condominium", and the name of the association.

2. The name of every county in which any portion of the condominium is located.

3. A legal description of the real estate included in the condominium.

4. Description of the boundaries of each unit created by the declaration, including each unit's identifying number.

5. A description of any limited common elements, other than those specified in section 33-1212, paragraphs 2 and 4, but the declaration shall contain a description of any porches, balconies, patios and entryways, if any, as provided in section 33-1219, subsection B, paragraph 11.

6. A description of any development rights and other special declarant rights, together with a legal description of the real estate to which each of those rights applies, any time limit within which each of those rights must be exercised and any other conditions or limitations under which the rights described in this paragraph may be exercised or will lapse.

7. An allocation to each unit of the allocated interests in the manner described in section 33-1217.

8. Any restrictions on use, occupancy and alienation of the units.

9. All matters required by sections 33-1216, 33-1217, 33-1218, 33-1219 and 33-1226 and section 33-1243, subsection E.

10. A statement that the assessment obligation of the unit owner under section 33-1255 is secured by a lien on the owner's unit in favor of the association pursuant to section 33-1256.

11. If the condominium is a conversion from multifamily rental to condominiums, a statement containing all of the following:

   a) A statement that the property is a conversion from multifamily rental to condominiums.

   b) The date original construction was completed.

   c) The name and address of the original owner, builder, developer and general contractor as shown on the applicable city, town or county building permit.

   d) The name and address of each subsequent owner as determined by a search of the county recorder's records in the county in which the property is located.

e) The sub divider's agreement to provide the following information on request:

f) The name and address of any builder, developer, general contractor, subcontractor, architect and engineer who designed or made improvements to the property immediately before the first condominium was sold.

g) A specific description of all improvements made.

B. If a city, town or county is unable to produce a building permit as required in subsection A, paragraph 11, subdivision (c) of this section, the sub divider shall submit a letter from the applicable city, town or county stating that the information required by subsection A, paragraph 11, subdivision (c) of this section is not available.

C. The declaration may contain any other matters the declarant deems appropriate.

33-1216. Leasehold Condominiums

A. Any lease, the expiration or termination of which may terminate the condominium or reduce its size, shall be recorded. Unless the lease otherwise specifically provides for the creation of a leasehold condominium and the rights and benefits set forth in this section, each lessor of those leases shall sign or otherwise consent to the provisions of the declaration. The declaration shall state all of the following:

1. The recording data for the lease.

2. The date on which the lease is scheduled to expire.

3. A legal description of the real estate subject to the lease.

4. Any right of the unit owners to acquire title to their units free of the lease or a statement that they do not have this right.

5. Any right of the unit owners to remove any improvements within a reasonable time after the expiration or termination of the lease or that they do not have this right.

6. Any rights of the unit owners to renew the lease and the conditions of any renewal or that they do not have those rights.

B. After the declaration for a leasehold condominium is recorded, neither the lessor nor his successor in interest may terminate the leasehold interest of a unit owner who makes timely payment of his share of the rent and otherwise complies with all covenants which, if violated, would entitle the lessor to terminate the lease. A unit owner's leasehold interest is not affected by failure of any other person to pay rent or fulfill any other covenant.

C. Acquisition of the leasehold interest of any unit owner by the owner of the reversion or remainder does not merge the leasehold and fee simple interests unless the leasehold interests of all unit owners subject to that reversion or remainder are acquired.

D. If the expiration or termination of a lease decreases the number of units in a condominium, the allocated interests shall be reallocated in accordance with section 33-1206, subsection A as though those units had been taken by eminent domain.

33-1217. Allocations of Common Element Interests, Votes and Common Expense Liabilities

A. The declaration shall allocate a fraction or percentage of undivided interests in the common elements and in the common expenses of the association, and a portion of the votes in the association, to each unit and state the formulas used to establish those allocations. Except as otherwise provided in this chapter, the allocations shall not discriminate in favor of units owned by the declarant.

B. If units may be added to or withdrawn from the condominium, the declaration must state the formulas to be used to reallocate the allocated interests among all units included in the condominium after the addition or withdrawal.

C. The declaration may provide:

1. That different allocations of votes shall be made to the units on particular matters specified in the declaration.

2. For cumulative voting only for the purpose of electing members of the board of directors.

3. For class voting on specified issues affecting the class if necessary to protect valid interests of the class.

D. Except for minor variations due to rounding, the sum of the undivided interests in the common elements and common expense liabilities allocated at any time to all the units must each equal one if stated as fractions or one hundred per cent if stated as percentages. If a discrepancy exists between an allocated interest and the result derived from application of the pertinent formula, the allocated interest prevails.

E. Except as otherwise permitted by the provisions of this chapter, the common elements are not subject to partition, and any purported conveyance, encumbrance, judicial sale or other voluntary or involuntary transfer of an undivided interest in the common elements made without the unit to which that interest is allocated is void.

33-1218. Limited Common Elements

A. Except for the limited common elements described in section 33-1212, paragraphs 2 and 4, other than porches, balconies, patios and entryways, the declaration shall specify to which unit or units each limited common element is allocated. The allocation shall not be altered without the consent of the unit owners whose units are affected.

B. Except as the declaration otherwise provides, a limited common element may be reallocated by an amendment to the declaration. The amendment shall be executed by the unit owners between or among whose units the reallocation is made, shall state the manner in which the limited common elements are to be reallocated and, before recording the amendment, shall be submitted to the board of directors. Unless the board of directors determines within thirty days that the proposed amendment is unreasonable, which determination shall be in writing and specifically state the reasons for disapproval, the association shall execute its approval and record the amendment.

C. A common element not previously allocated as a limited common element shall not be so allocated except pursuant to provisions in the declaration. The allocations shall be made by amendments to the declaration.

33-1219. Plat

A. The plat is a part of the declaration. The plat must be clear and legible.

B. The plat shall show:

1. The name of the condominium.

2 .The boundaries of the condominium and a legal description of the real estate included in the condominium.

3. The extent of any encroachments on any portion of the condominium.

4. To the extent feasible, the location and dimensions of all easements serving or burdening any portion of the condominium.

5. The location and dimensions of the vertical boundaries of each unit, and each unit's identifying number.

6. Any horizontal unit boundaries, with reference to an established datum, and each unit's identifying number.

7. Any units with respect to which the declarant has reserved the right to create additional units or common elements, identified appropriately.

8. The location and dimensions of all real estate subject to the development right of withdrawal identified as such.

9. The location and dimensions of all real estate in which the unit owner will only own an estate for years labeled as a " leasehold condominium".

10. The distance between noncontiguous parcels of real estate comprising the condominium.

11. The location and dimensions of limited common elements, including porches, balconies, patios and entryways, other than the limited common elements described in section 33-1212, paragraphs 2 and 4.

12. Any other matters the declarant deems appropriate.

C. Unless the declaration provides otherwise, the horizontal boundaries of a part of a unit located outside of a building have the same elevation as the horizontal boundaries of the inside part and need not be depicted on the plat

D. On exercising any development right, the declarant shall record a new plat conforming to the requirements of subsections A and B of this section. No new plat need be recorded if the development right exercised was clearly depicted on the original plat and a document is recorded which references the declaration and original plat and declares that the development right has been exercised.

33-1220. Exercise of Development Rights

A. To exercise a development right the declarant shall prepare, execute and record an amendment to the declaration which shall include a new plat conforming to the requirements of section 33-1219, subsections A and B, if the previously recorded plat does not show the boundaries of the parcel or parcels as to which the development right is exercised. The amendment to the declaration shall assign an identifying number to each new unit created and, except in the case of subdivision or conversion of units described in subsection C of this section, reallocate the allocated interests among all units. The amendment shall describe any common elements and any limited common elements created and, in the case of limited common elements, designate the unit to which each is allocated as required by section 33-1218.

B. Development rights may be reserved within any real estate added to the condominium if the amendment adding that real estate includes all matters required by section 33-1215 or 33-1216, whichever is applicable, and the plat includes all matters required by section 33-1219. This subsection does not extend any time limit on the exercise of development rights imposed by the declaration pursuant to section 33-1215, subsection A, paragraph 6.

C. Whenever a declarant exercises a development right to subdivide or convert a unit previously created into additional units or common elements, or both:

1. If the declarant converts the unit entirely too common elements, the amendment to the declaration must reallocate all the allocated interests of that unit among the other units as if that unit had been taken by eminent domain.

2. If the declarant subdivides the unit into two or more units, whether any part of the unit is converted into common elements, the amendment to the declaration shall reallocate all

61

the allocated interests of the unit among the units created by the subdivision in any reasonable manner prescribed by the declarant.

D. If the declaration provides that all or a portion of the real estate is subject to the development right of withdrawal:

1. If all the real estate is subject to withdrawal and the declaration does not describe separate portions of the real estate subject to that right, none of the real estate may be withdrawn after a unit has been conveyed to a purchaser without the written consent of all unit owners in the condominium and any mortgagees or beneficiaries of deeds of trust or sellers under a contract, as defined in section 33-741, for conveyance of real property encumbering the units.

2. If a portion or portions are subject to withdrawal, a portion shall not be withdrawn after a unit in that portion has been conveyed to a purchaser without the written consent of all unit owners in the condominium and any mortgagees or beneficiaries of deeds of trust or sellers under contract, as defined in section 33-741, for conveyance of real property encumbering the units.

E. No development right shall be exercised in any manner which would eliminate or materially reduce in size any tennis court, swimming pool, clubhouse or other recreational facility which is part of the common elements and which was specified in the public report issued on the condominium by the commissioner of the state real estate department, unless the exercise of the development right is approved by an affirmative vote of the unit owners to which at least eighty per cent of the votes in the association are allocated.

33-1221. Alterations of Units

Subject to the provisions of the declaration and other provisions of law, a unit owner:

1. May make any improvements or alterations to his unit that do not impair the structural integrity or mechanical systems or lessen the support of any portion of the condominium.

2. Shall not change the appearance of the common elements, or the exterior appearance of a unit or any other portion of the condominium, without written permission of the association.

3. After acquiring an adjoining unit or, if the declaration expressly permits, an adjoining part of an adjoining unit, may remove or alter any intervening partition or create apertures in intervening partitions, even if the partition in whole or in part is a common element, if those acts do not impair the structural integrity or mechanical systems or lessen the support of any portion of the condominium. Removal of partitions or creation of apertures under this paragraph is not an alteration of boundaries.

33-1222. Relocation of Boundaries Between Adjoining Units

If the declaration expressly permits, the boundaries between or among adjoining units may be relocated by an amendment to the declaration. The owners of the units shall prepare an amendment to the declaration, including the plat that identifies the units involved, specifies the altered boundaries of the units and their dimensions and includes the units' identifying numbers. If the owners of the adjoining units have specified a reallocation between their units of the allocated interests, the amendment shall state the proposed reallocation in a reasonable manner. The amendment shall be executed by the owners of those units, shall contain words of conveyance between or among them and, before recording the amendment, shall be submitted to the board of directors. Unless the board of directors determines within thirty days that the proposed amendment is unreasonable, which determination shall be in writing and specifically state the reasons for disapproval, the association shall execute its approval and record the amendment.

33-1223. Subdivision of Units

If the declaration expressly permits, a unit may be subdivided into two or more units. A unit owner shall prepare an amendment to the declaration, including the plat, which identifies the unit involved, specifies the boundaries of each unit created and its dimensions, assigns an identifying number to each unit created and allocates the allocated interests formerly allocated to the subdivided unit to the new units in a reasonable manner. The amendment shall be executed by the owner of the unit to be subdivided and, before recording, submitted to the board of directors. Unless the board of directors determines within thirty days that the proposed amendment is unreasonable, which determination shall be in writing and specifically state the reasons for disapproval, the association shall execute its approval and record the amendment.

33-1224. Easement for Encroachments

To the extent that any unit or common element encroaches on any other unit or common element as a result of original construction, shifting or settling, or alteration or restoration authorized by the declaration, a valid easement for the encroachment exists.

33-1225. Use for Sale Purposes

A. Declarant may maintain sales offices, management offices and models in units or on common elements in the condominium unless:

1. The declaration provides otherwise.

2. Such use is prohibited by another provision of law or local ordinances.

33-1226. Easement to Facilitate Exercise of Special Declarant Rights

Subject to the provisions of the declaration, a declarant has an easement through the common elements as may be reasonably necessary for the purpose of discharging a declarant's obligations or exercising special declarant rights, whether arising under this chapter or reserved in the declaration.

33-1227. Amendment of Declaration

A. Except in cases of amendments that may be executed by a declarant under section 33-1220, by the association under section 33-1206 or section 33-1216, subsection D, or by certain unit owners under section 33-1218, subsection B, section 33-1222, section 33-1223 or section 33-1228, subsection B, and except to the extent permitted or required by other provisions of this chapter, the declaration, including the plat, may be amended only by a vote of the unit owners to which at least sixty-seven per cent of the votes in the association are allocated, or any larger majority the declaration specifies. The declaration may specify a smaller percentage only if all of the units are restricted exclusively to nonresidential use. The declaration may also provide that the consent of the declarant is required to an amendment during any period of declarant control pursuant to section 33-1243. Within thirty days after the adoption of any amendment pursuant to this subsection, the association shall prepare, execute and record a written instrument setting forth the amendment.

B. An action to challenge the validity of an amendment adopted by the association pursuant to this section shall not be brought more than one year after the amendment is recorded.

C. An amendment to the declaration shall be recorded in each county in which any portion of the condominium is located and is effective only on recordation in the same manner as required for the declaration under section 33-1211.

D. Except to the extent expressly permitted or required by other provisions of this chapter, an amendment shall not create or increase special declarant rights, increase the number of units or change the boundaries of any unit, the allocated interests of a unit or the uses to which any unit is restricted, in the absence of unanimous consent of the unit owners.

E. An amendment shall not terminate or decrease any unexpired development right, special declarant right or period of declarant control unless the declarant approves.

F. Amendments to the declaration required by this chapter to be executed by the association shall be executed on behalf of the association by any officer of the association designated for that purpose or, in the absence of designation, by the president of the association.

33-1228. Termination of Condominium

A. Except in the case of a taking of all the units by eminent domain, a condominium may be terminated only by agreement of unit owners of units to which at least eighty per cent of the votes in the association are allocated, or any larger percentage the declaration specifies. The declaration may specify a smaller percentage only if all of the units in the condominium are restricted exclusively to nonresidential uses.

B. An agreement to terminate shall be evidenced by the execution or ratifications of a termination agreement, in the same manner as a deed, by the requisite number of unit owners. The termination agreement shall specify a date after which the agreement will be void unless it is recorded before that date. A termination agreement and all ratifications of a termination agreement shall be recorded in each county in which a portion of the condominium is situated and is effective only on recordation.

C. A termination agreement may provide that all the common elements and units of the condominium shall be sold following termination. If, pursuant to the agreement, any real estate in the condominium is to be sold following termination, the termination agreement shall set forth the minimum terms of the sale.

D. The association, on behalf of the unit owners, may contract for the sale of real estate in the condominium, but the contract is not binding on the unit owners until approved pursuant to subsections A and B. If any real estate in the condominium is to be sold following termination, title to that real estate on termination vests in the association as trustee for the holders of all interest in the units. Thereafter, the association has all powers necessary and appropriate to effect the sale. Until the sale has been concluded and the proceeds of the sale distributed, the association continues in existence with all powers it had before termination. Proceeds of the sale shall be distributed to unit owners and lienholders as their interests may appear, in proportion to the respective interests of unit owners as provided in subsection G. Unless otherwise specified in the termination agreement, as long as the association holds title to the real estate, each unit owner and his successors in interest have an exclusive right to occupancy of the portion of the real estate that formerly constituted his unit. During the period of that occupancy, each unit owner and his successors in interest remain liable for all assessments and other obligations imposed on unit owners by this chapter or the declaration.

E. If the real estate constituting the condominium is not to be sold following termination, title to all the real estate in the condominium vests in the unit owners on termination as tenants in common in proportion to their respective interests as provided in subsection G, and liens on the units shift accordingly. While the tenancy in common exists, each unit owner and his successors in interest have an exclusive right to occupancy of the portion of the real estate that formerly constituted his unit.

F. Following termination of the condominium, the proceeds of any sale of real estate, together with the assets of the association, are held by the association as trustee for unit owners and holders of liens on the units as their interests may appear. Following termination, creditors of the association holding liens on the units which were recorded before termination may enforce those liens in the same manner as any lienholder.

G. The respective interests of unit owners referred to in subsections D, E and F are as follows:

   1. Except as provided in paragraph 2, the respective interests of unit owners are the fair market values of their units, limited common elements and common element interests immediately before the termination, as determined by an independent appraiser selected by the association. The determination of the independent appraiser shall be distributed to the unit owners and becomes final unless disapproved within thirty days after distribution by unit owners of units to which fifty per cent of the votes in the association are allocated. The proportion of any unit owner's interest to that of all unit owners is determined by dividing the fair market value of that unit owner's unit and common element interest by the total fair market values of all the units and common elements.

   2. If any unit or any limited common element is destroyed to the extent that an appraisal of the fair market value of the unit or element before destruction cannot be made, the interests of all unit owners are their respective common element interests immediately before the termination.

H. Except as provided in subsection I, foreclosure or enforcement of a lien or encumbrance against the entire condominium does not of itself terminate the condominium, and foreclosure or enforcement of a lien or encumbrance against a portion of the condominium does not withdraw that portion from the condominium.

Foreclosure or enforcement of a lien or encumbrance against withdrawable real estate does not of itself withdraw that real estate from the condominium, but the person taking title may require from the association, on request, an amendment excluding the real estate from the condominium.

I. If a lien or encumbrance against a portion of the real estate comprising the condominium has priority over the declaration, and the lien or encumbrance has not been partially released, the parties foreclosing the lien or encumbrance may, on foreclosure, record an instrument excluding the real estate subject to that lien or encumbrance from the condominium.

J. The provisions of subsections C through I do not apply if the original declaration, an amendment to the original declaration recorded before the conveyance of any unit to an owner other than the declarant or an agreement by all of the unit owners contain provisions inconsistent with such subsections.

33-1229. Rights of Secured Lenders

The declaration may require that all or a specified number or percentage of the mortgagees, beneficiaries of deeds of trust or sellers under contracts, as defined in section 33-741, for conveyance of real property encumbering the units approve specified actions of the unit owners or the association as a condition to the effectiveness of those actions, but requirement for approval shall not operate to either:

1. Deny or delegate control over the general administrative affairs of the association by the unit owners or the board of directors.

2. Prevent the association or the board of directors from commencing, intervening in or settling any litigation or proceeding, or receiving and distributing any insurance proceeds pursuant to section 33-1253.

33-1230. Merger or Consolidation of Condominiums

A. Any two or more condominiums, by agreement of the unit owners as provided in subsection B, may be merged or consolidated into a single condominium. In the event of a merger or consolidation, unless the agreement otherwise provides, the resultant condominium is, for all purposes, the legal successor of all of the preexisting condominiums and the operations and activities of all associations of the preexisting condominiums shall be merged or consolidated into a single association which shall hold all powers, rights, obligations, assets and liabilities of all preexisting associations.

B. An agreement of two or more condominiums to merge or consolidate pursuant to subsection A shall be evidenced by an agreement prepared, executed, recorded and certified by the president of the association of each of the preexisting condominiums following approval by owners of units to which are allocated the percentage of votes in each condominium required to terminate that condominium. Any such agreement shall be recorded in each county in which a portion of the condominium is located and is not effective until recorded. A merger or consolidation of two or more condominiums shall be considered an amendment to the declaration of each of the condominiums merged or consolidated.

C. Every merger or consolidation agreement shall provide for the reallocation of the allocated interests in the new association among the units of the resultant condominium either by stating:

   1. The reallocations or the formulas on which they are based.

   2. The percentage of overall allocated interests of the new condominium which are allocated to all of the units comprising each of the preexisting condominiums, and providing that the portion of the percentages allocated to each unit formerly comprising a part of the preexisting condominium must be equal to the percentages of allocated interests allocated to that unit by the declaration of the preexisting condominiums.

33-1241. Organization of Unit-owners' Association

A unit owners' association shall be organized no later than the date the first unit in the condominium is conveyed. The membership of the association at all times shall consist exclusively of all the unit owners or, following termination of the condominium, of all former unit owners entitled to distributions of proceeds under section 33-

1228, or their heirs, successors or assigns. The association shall be organized as a profit or nonprofit corporation or as an unincorporated association.

33-1242. Powers of Unit-owners' Association; Notice to Unit-owner of Violation

A. Subject to the provisions of the declaration, the association may:

1. Adopt and amend bylaws and rules.

2. Adopt and amend budgets for revenues, expenditures and reserves and collect assessments for common expenses from unit owners.

3. Hire and discharge managing agents and other employees, agents and independent contractors.

4 Institute, defend or intervene in litigation or administrative proceedings in its own name on behalf of itself or two or more unit owners on matters affecting the condominium.

5. Make contracts and incur liabilities.

6. Regulate the use, maintenance, repair, replacement and modification of common elements.

7. Cause additional improvements to be made as a part of the common elements.

8. Acquire, hold, encumber and convey in its own name any right, title or interest to real or personal property, except that common elements may be conveyed or subjected to a security interest only pursuant to section 33-1252.

9. Grant easements, leases, licenses and concessions through or over the common elements.

10. Impose and receive any payments, fees or charges for the use, rental or operation of the common elements other than limited common elements described in section 33-1212, paragraphs 2 and 4 and for services provided to unit owners.

11. Impose charges for late payment of assessments and, after notice and an opportunity to be heard, impose reasonable monetary penalties upon unit owners for violations of the declaration, bylaws and rules of the association.

12. Impose reasonable charges for the preparation and recordation of amendments to the declaration or statements of unpaid assessments.

13. Provide for the indemnification of its officers and executive board of directors and maintain directors' and officers' liability insurance.

14. Assign its right to future income, including the right to receive common expense assessments, but only to the extent the declaration expressly provides.

15. Be a member of a master association or other entity owning, maintaining or governing in any respect any portion of the common elements or other property benefitting or related to the condominium or the unit owners in any respect.

16. Exercise any other powers conferred by the declaration or bylaws.

17. Exercise all other powers that may be exercised in this state by legal entities of the same type as the association.

18. Exercise any other powers necessary and proper for the governance and operation of the association.

B. A unit owner who receives a written notice that the condition of the property owned by the unit owner is in violation of a requirement of the condominium documents without regard to whether a monetary penalty is imposed by the notice may provide the association with a written response by sending the response by certified mail within ten business days after the date of the notice. The response shall be sent to the address contained in the notice or in the recorded notice prescribed by section 33-1256, subsection J. Within ten business days after receipt of the certified mail containing the response from the unit owner, the association shall respond to the unit owner with a written explanation regarding the notice that shall provide at least the following information unless previously provided in the notice of violation:

1. The provision of the condominium documents that has allegedly been violated.

2. The date of the violation or the date the violation was observed.

3. The first and last name of the person or persons who observed the violation.

4. The process the unit owner must follow to contest the notice.

> (UPDATE: Effective late in 2016, an additional grace period will be given to homeowners responding to a notice of violation. Homeowners will now be given 21 calendar days to provide the HOA with a written response: thanks to attorney Patrick MacQueen, Combs, Gottlieb & Gottlieb, P.C.)

C. Unless the information required in subsection C, paragraph 4 of this section is provided in the notice of violation, the association shall not proceed with any action to enforce the condominium documents, including the collection of attorney fees, before or during the time prescribed by subsection C of this section regarding the exchange of information between the association and the unit owner. At any time before or after completion of the exchange of information pursuant to this section, the unit owner may petition for a hearing pursuant to section 41-2198.01 if the dispute is within the jurisdiction of the department of fire, building and life safety as prescribed in section 41-2198.01, subsection B.

33-1243. Board of Directors and Officers; Conflict; Powers; Limitations; Removal; Annual Audit; Applicability

A. Except as provided in the declaration, the bylaws, subsection B or other provisions of this chapter, the board of directors may act in all instances on behalf of the association.

B. The board of directors shall not act on behalf of the association to amend the declaration, terminate the condominium, elect members of the board of directors or determine the qualifications, powers and duties or terms of office of board of director's members. The board of directors may fill vacancies in its membership for the unexpired portion of any term.

C. If any contract, decision or other action for compensation taken by or on behalf of the board of directors would benefit any member of the board of directors or any person who is a parent, grandparent, spouse, child or sibling of a member of the board of directors or a parent or spouse of any of those persons, that member of the board of directors shall declare a conflict of interest for that issue. The member shall declare the conflict in an open meeting of the board before the board discusses or takes action on that issue and that member may then vote on that issue. Any contract entered into in violation of this subsection is void and unenforceable.

D. Except as provided in the declaration, within thirty days after adoption of any proposed budget for the condominium, the board of directors shall provide a summary of the budget to all the unit owners. Unless the board of directors is expressly authorized in the declaration to adopt and amend budgets from time to time, any budget or amendment shall be ratified by the unit owners in accordance with the procedures set forth in this subsection. If ratification is required, the board of directors shall set a date for a meeting of the unit owners to consider ratification of the budget not fewer than fourteen nor more than thirty days after mailing of the summary. Unless at that meeting a majority of all the unit owners or any larger vote specified in the declaration rejects the budget, the budget is ratified, whether or not a quorum is present. If the proposed budget is rejected, the periodic budget last ratified by the unit owners shall be continued until such time as the unit owners ratify a subsequent budget proposed by the board of directors.

E. The declaration may provide for a period of declarant control of the association, during which period a declarant or persons designated by the declarant may appoint and remove the officers and members of the board of directors. Regardless of the period provided in the declaration, a period of declarant control terminates no later than the earlier of:

1. Ninety days after conveyance of seventy-five per cent of the units which may be created to unit owners other than a declarant.

2. Four years after all declarants have ceased to offer units for sale in the ordinary course of business.

F. A declarant may voluntarily surrender the right to appoint and remove officers and members of the board of directors before termination of the period prescribed in subsection E, but in that event the declarant may require, for the duration of the period of declarant control, that specified actions of the association or board of directors, as described in a recorded instrument executed by the declarant, be approved by the declarant before they become effective.

G. Not later than the termination of any period of declarant control the unit owners shall elect a board of directors of at least three members, at least a majority of whom must be unit owners. The board of directors shall elect the officers. The board members and officers shall take office upon election.

H. Notwithstanding any provision of the declaration or bylaws to the contrary, the unit owners, by a majority vote of members entitled to vote and voting on the matter at a meeting of the members called pursuant to this section at which a quorum is present, may remove any member of the board of directors with or without cause, other than a member appointed by the declarant. For purposes of calling for removal of a member of the board of directors, other than a member appointed by the declarant, the following apply:

1. In an association with one thousand or fewer members, on receipt of a petition that calls for removal of a member of the board of directors and that is signed by the number of persons who are entitled to cast at least twenty-five per cent of the votes in the association or one hundred votes in the association, whichever is less, the board shall call and provide written notice of a special meeting of the association as prescribed by section 33-1248, subsection B.

2. Notwithstanding section 33-1248, subsection B, in an association with more than one thousand members, on receipt of a petition that calls for removal of a member of the board of directors and that is signed by the number of persons who are entitled to cast at least ten per cent of the votes in the association or one thousand votes in the association, whichever is less, the board shall call and provide written notice of a special meeting of the association. The board shall provide written notice of a special meeting as prescribed by section 33-1248, subsection B.

74

3. The special meeting shall be called, noticed and held within thirty days after receipt of the petition.

4. For purposes of a special meeting called pursuant to this subsection, a quorum is present if the number of owners to whom at least twenty per cent of the votes or one thousand votes, whichever is less, are allocated is present at the meeting in person or as otherwise permitted by law.

   a) In an association with one thousand or fewer members, on receipt of a petition that calls for removal of a member of the board of directors and that is signed by the number of persons who are eligible to vote in the association at the time the person signs the petition equal to at least twenty-five percent of the votes in the association or by the number of persons who are eligible to vote in the association at the time the person signs the petition equal to at least one hundred votes in the association, whichever is less, the board shall call and provide written notice of a special meeting of the association as prescribed by section 33-1248, subsection B.

   b) Notwithstanding section 33-1248, subsection B, in an association with more than one thousand members, on receipt of a petition that calls for removal of a member of the board of directors and that is signed by the number of persons who are eligible to vote in the association at the time the person signs the petition equal to at least ten percent of the votes in the association or by the number of persons who are eligible to vote in the association at the time the person signs the petition equal to at least one thousand votes in the association, whichever is less, the board shall call and provide written notice of a special meeting of the association. The board shall provide written notice of a special meeting as prescribed by section 33-1248, subsection B.

   c) The special meeting shall be called, noticed and held within thirty days after receipt of the petition.

   d) For purposes of a special meeting called pursuant to this subsection, a quorum is present if the number of owners who are eligible to vote in the association at the time the person attends the meeting equal to at least twenty percent of the votes of the association or the number of persons who are eligible to vote in the association at the time the person attends the meeting equal to at least one thousand votes, whichever is less, is present at the meeting in person or as otherwise permitted by law.

e) If a civil action is filed regarding the removal of a board member, the prevailing party in the civil action shall be awarded its reasonable attorney fees and costs.

f) The board of directors shall retain all documents and other records relating to the proposed removal of the member of the board of directors and any election or other action taken for that director's replacement for at least one year after the date of the special meeting and shall permit members to inspect those documents and records pursuant to section 33-1258.

g) A petition that calls for the removal of the same member of the board of directors shall not be submitted more than once during each term of office for that member.

5. If a civil action is filed regarding the removal of a board member, the prevailing party in the civil action shall be awarded its reasonable attorney fees and costs.

6. The board of directors shall retain all documents and other records relating to the proposed removal of the member of the board of directors for at least one year after the date of the special meeting and shall permit members to inspect those documents and records pursuant to section 33-1258.

7. A petition that calls for the removal of the same member of the board of directors shall not be submitted more than once during each term of office for that member.

I. For an association in which board members are elected from separately designated voting districts, a member of the board of directors, other than a member appointed by the declarant, may be removed only by a vote of the members from that voting district, and only the members from that voting district are eligible to vote on the matter or be counted for purposes of determining a quorum.

J. Unless any provision in the condominium documents requires an annual audit by a certified public accountant, the board of directors shall provide for an annual financial audit, review or compilation of the association. The audit, review or compilation shall be completed no later than one hundred eighty days after the end of the association's fiscal year and shall be made available upon request to the unit owners within thirty days after its completion.

K. This section does not apply to timeshare plans or associations, or the period of declarant control under timeshare instruments that are subject to chapter 20 of this title.

33-1244. Transfer of special declarant rights

A. A special declarant right created or reserved under this chapter shall not be transferred except by an instrument evidencing the transfer recorded in every county in which any portion of the condominium is located. The instrument is not effective unless executed by the transferee.

B. On transfer of any special declarant right, the liability of a transferor declarant is as follows:

1. A transferor is not relieved of any obligation or liability arising before the transfer.

2. If a transferor retains any special declarant right, the transferor is liable for any obligations or liabilities imposed on a declarant by this chapter or by the declaration relating to the retained special declarant rights and arising after the transfer.

3. A transferor has no liability for any act or omission or any breach of a contractual or warranty obligation arising from the exercise of a special declarant right by a successor declarant.

C. Unless otherwise provided in a mortgage or deed of trust, in case of foreclosure of a mortgage, tax sale, judicial sale, sale by a trustee under a deed of trust, forfeiture of interest of a purchaser under a contract for conveyance of real property or sale under bankruptcy code or receivership proceedings, of any units owned by a declarant or real estate in a condominium subject to development rights, a person acquiring title to all the real estate being foreclosed or sold succeeds to all special declarant rights related to that real estate held by that declarant whether or not the judgment or instrument conveying title provides for transfer of the special declarant rights.

D. The liabilities and obligations of a person who succeeds to special declarant rights are as follows:

1. A successor to any special declarant right, other than a successor described in paragraph 2 of this subsection, is subject to all liabilities and obligations imposed by this chapter or the declaration:

   a) On a declarant which relate to his exercise or non exercise of special declarant rights.

   b) On his transferor, other than:

      i. Misrepresentations by any previous declarant.

      ii Warranty obligations on improvements made by any previous declarant or made before the condominium was created.

      iii. Breach of any fiduciary obligation by any previous declarant or his appointees to the board of directors.

      iv. Any liability or obligation imposed on the transferor as a result of the transferor's acts or omissions after the transfer.

2. A successor to special declarant rights under subsection C is subject to liability only for his own acts in the exercise of those special declarant rights.

33-1245. Termination of contracts and leases of declarant; applicability

A. A contract for any of the following, if entered into before the board of directors elected by the unit owners pursuant to section 33-1243, subsection G takes office, shall contain a provision in the contract that the contract may be terminated without penalty by the association at any time after the board of directors elected by the unit owners takes office:

   1. Any management contract or employment contract.

   2. Any other contract or lease between the association and a declarant or an affiliate of a declarant.

   3. Any contract or lease that is not bona fide or was unconscionable to the unit owners at the time entered into under the circumstances then prevailing.

B. The board of directors shall notify the appropriate contractual party of the termination at least thirty days before termination.

C. Lease would terminate the condominium or reduce its size.

D. If a contract covered by this section fails to contain the provisions required by subsection A of this section, the contract is voidable at the option of the association.

E. This section does not apply to timeshare plans or associations that are subject to chapter 20 of this title.

33-1246. Bylaws

A. At the time the unit owners' association is organized, the association shall adopt bylaws, which provide for each of the following:

1. The number of members of the board of directors and the titles of the officers of the association.

2. Election by the board of directors of a president, treasurer, secretary and any other officers of the association which the bylaws specify.

3. The qualifications, powers and duties, terms of office and manner of electing and removing board members and officers and filling vacancies.

4. Which, if any, of its powers the board of directors or officers may delegate to other persons or to a managing agent.

5. Which of its officers may execute, certify and record amendments to the declaration on behalf of the association.

6. The method of amending the bylaws.

B. Subject to the provisions of the declaration, the bylaws may provide for any other matters the association deems necessary and appropriate.

33-1247. Upkeep of the condominium

A. Except to the extent provided by the declaration, subsection C of this section or section 33-1253, subsection B, the association is responsible for maintenance, repair and replacement of the common elements and each unit owner is responsible for maintenance, repair and replacement of the unit. On reasonable notice, each unit owner shall afford to the association and the other unit owners, and to their agents or employees, access through the unit reasonably necessary for those purposes. If damage is inflicted on the common elements or any unit through which access is taken, the unit owner responsible for the damage, or the association if it is responsible, is liable for the prompt repair of the damage.

B. For any residential rental units that have been declared a slum property by the city or town pursuant to section 33-1905 and that are in the condominium complex, the association is responsible for enforcing any requirement for a licensed property management firm that is imposed by a city or town pursuant to section 33-1906.

C. In addition to the liability borne by the declarant as a unit owner under this chapter, the declarant alone is liable for the maintenance, repair and replacement of any portion of the common elements which the declarant reserves the right to withdraw from the condominium, as long as the unit owner maintains that right.

33-1248. Open meetings; exceptions

A. Notwithstanding any provision in the declaration, bylaws or other documents to the contrary, all meetings of the unit owners' association and the board of directors, and any regularly scheduled committee meetings, are open to all members of the association or any person designated by a member in writing as the member's representative and all members or designated representatives so desiring shall be permitted to attend and speak at an appropriate time during the deliberations and proceedings. The board may place reasonable time restrictions on those persons speaking during the meeting but shall permit a member or a member's designated representative to speak once after the board has discussed a specific agenda item but before the board takes formal action on that item in addition to any other opportunities to speak. The board shall provide for a reasonable number of persons to speak on each side of an issue. Persons attending may audiotape or videotape those portions of the meetings of the board of directors and meetings of the members that are open. The board of directors of the association may adopt reasonable rules governing the audiotaping or videotaping of open portions of the meetings of the board and the membership, but such rules shall not preclude such audiotaping or videotaping by those attending. Any portion of a meeting may be closed only if that portion of the meeting is limited to consideration of one or more of the following:

1. Legal advice from an attorney for the board or the association. On final resolution of any matter for which the board received legal advice or that concerned pending or contemplated litigation, the board may disclose information about that matter in an open meeting except for matters that are required to remain confidential by the terms of a settlement agreement or judgment.

2. Pending or contemplated litigation.

3. Personal, health or financial information about an individual member of the association, an individual employee of the association or an individual employee of a contractor for the association, including records of the association directly related to the personal, health or financial information about an individual member of the association, an individual employee of the association or an individual employee of a contractor for the association.

4. Matters relating to the job performance of, compensation of, health records of or specific complaints against an individual employee of the association or an individual employee of a contractor of the association who works under the direction of the association.

5. Discussion of a unit owner's appeal of any violation cited or penalty imposed by the association except on request of the affected unit owner that the meeting be held in an open session.

B. Notwithstanding any provision in the condominium documents, all meetings of the unit owners' association and the board shall be held in this state. A meeting of the unit owners' association shall be held at least once each year. Special meetings of the unit owners' association may be called by the president, by a majority of the board of directors or by unit owners having at least twenty-five per cent, or any lower percentage specified in the bylaws, of the votes in the association. Not fewer than ten nor more than fifty days in advance of any meeting of the unit owners, the secretary shall cause notice to be hand delivered or sent prepaid by United States mail to the mailing address of each unit or to any other mailing address designated in writing by the unit owner. The notice of any meeting of the unit owners shall state the time and place of the meeting. The notice of any special meeting of the unit owners shall also state the purpose for which the meeting is called, including the general nature of any proposed amendment to the declaration or bylaws, any changes in assessments that require approval of the unit owners and any proposal to remove a director or officer. The failure of any unit owner to receive actual notice of a meeting of the unit owners does not affect the validity of any action taken at that meeting.

C. Notwithstanding any provision in the declaration, bylaws or other condominium documents, for meetings of the board of directors that are held after the termination of declarant control of the association, notice to unit owners of meetings of the board of directors shall be given at least forty-eight hours in advance of the meeting by newsletter, conspicuous posting or any other reasonable means as determined by the board of directors. An affidavit of notice by an officer of the association is prima facie evidence that notice was given as prescribed by this section. Notice to unit owners of meetings of the board of directors is not required if emergency circumstances require action by the board before notice can be given. Any notice of a board meeting shall state the time and place of the meeting. The failure of any unit owner to receive actual notice of a meeting of the board of directors does not affect the validity of any action taken at that meeting.

D. Notwithstanding any provision in the declaration, bylaws or other condominium documents, for meetings of the board of directors that are held after the termination of declarant control of the association, all of the following apply:

1. The agenda shall be available to all unit owners attending.

2. An emergency meeting of the board of directors may be called to discuss business or take action that cannot be delayed until the next regularly scheduled board meeting. The minutes of the emergency meeting shall state the reason necessitating the emergency meeting. The minutes of the emergency meeting shall be read and approved at the next regularly scheduled meeting of the board of directors.

3. A quorum of the board of directors may meet by means of a telephone conference if a speakerphone is available in the meeting room that allows board members and unit owners to hear all parties who are speaking during the meeting.

4. Any quorum of the board of directors that meets informally to discuss association business, including workshops, shall comply with the open meeting and notice provisions of this section without regard to whether the board votes or takes any action on any matter at that informal meeting.

E. It is the policy of this state as reflected in this section that all meetings of a condominium, whether meetings of the unit owners' association or meetings of the board of directors of the association, be conducted openly and that notices and agendas be provided for those meetings that contain the information that is reasonably necessary to inform the unit owners of the matters to be discussed or decided and to ensure that unit owners have the ability to speak after discussion of agenda items, but before a vote of the board of directors is taken. Toward this end, any person or entity that is charged with the interpretation of these provisions shall take into account this declaration of policy and shall construe any provision of this section in favor of open meetings.

F. This section does not apply to timeshare plans or associations that are subject to chapter 20 of this title.

33-1249. Quorums; applicability

A. Unless the bylaws provide otherwise, a quorum is present throughout any meeting of the association if persons entitled to cast at least twenty-five per cent of the votes in the association are present in person or by proxy at the beginning of the meeting.

B. Unless the bylaws specify a larger percentage, a quorum is deemed present throughout any meeting of the board of directors if persons entitled to cast at least fifty per cent of the votes on that board are present at the beginning of the meeting.

C. This section does not apply to timeshare plans or associations that are subject to chapter 20 of this title.

33-1250. Voting; proxies; absentee ballots; applicability; definition

A. If only one of the multiple owners of a unit is present at a meeting of the association, the owner is entitled to cast all the votes allocated to that unit. If more than one of the multiple owners are present, the votes allocated to that unit may be cast only in accordance with the agreement of a majority in interest of the multiple owners unless the declaration expressly provides otherwise. There is majority agreement if any one of the multiple owners casts the votes allocated to that unit without protest being made promptly to the person presiding over the meeting by any of the other owners of the unit.

B. During the period of declarant control, votes allocated to a unit may be cast pursuant to a proxy duly executed by a unit owner. If a unit is owned by more than one person, each owner of the unit may vote or register protest to the casting of votes by the other owners of the unit through a duly executed proxy. A unit owner may not revoke a proxy given pursuant to this section except by actual notice of revocation to the person presiding over a meeting of the association. A proxy is void if it is not dated or purports to be revocable without notice. The proxy is revoked on presentation of a later dated proxy executed by the same unit owner. A proxy terminates one year after its date, unless it specifies a shorter term or unless it states that it is coupled with an interest and is irrevocable.

C. Notwithstanding any provision in the condominium documents, after termination of the period of declarant control, votes allocated to a unit may not be cast pursuant to a proxy. The association shall provide for votes to be cast in person and by absentee ballot and, in addition, the association may provide for voting by some other form of delivery, including the use of electronic mail and facsimile delivery. Notwithstanding section 10-3708 or the provisions of the condominium documents, any action taken at an annual, regular or special meeting of the members shall comply with all of the following if absentee ballots or ballots provided by some other form of delivery are used:

1. The ballot shall set forth each proposed action.

2. The ballot shall provide an opportunity to vote for or against each proposed action.

3. The ballot is valid for only one specified election or meeting of the members and expires automatically after the completion of the election or meeting.

4. The ballot specifies the time and date by which the ballot must be delivered to the board of directors in order to be counted, which shall be at least seven days after the date that the board delivers the unvoted ballot to the member.

5. The ballot does not authorize another person to cast votes on behalf of the member.

D. Votes cast by absentee ballot or other form of delivery, including the use of electronic mail and facsimile delivery, are valid for the purpose of establishing a quorum.

E. Notwithstanding subsection C of this section, an association for a timeshare plan as defined in section 32-2197 may permit votes by a proxy that is duly executed by a unit owner.

F. If the declaration requires that votes on specified matters affecting the condominium be cast by lessees rather than unit owners of leased units all of the following apply:

  1. The provisions of subsections A and B of this section apply to lessees as if they were unit owners.

  2. Unit owners who have leased their units to other persons shall not cast votes on those specified matters.

  3. Lessees are entitled to notice of meetings, access to records and other rights respecting those matters as if they were unit owners. Unit owners shall also be given notice, in the manner prescribed in section 33-1248, of all meetings at which lessees may be entitled to vote.

G. Unless the declaration provides otherwise, votes allocated to a unit owned by the association shall not be cast.

H. This section does not apply to timeshare plans or associations that are subject to chapter 20 of this title.

I. For the purposes of this section, "period of declarant control" means the time during which the declarant or persons designated by the declarant may elect or appoint the members of the board of directors pursuant to the condominium documents or by virtue of superior voting power.

33-1251. Tort and contract liability

A. An action alleging a wrong done by the association shall be brought against the association and not against any unit owner.

B. A statute of limitation affecting any right of action of the association against the declarant is tolled until the period of declarant control terminates.

C. A unit owner is not precluded from bringing an action against the association because he is a unit owner or a member or officer of the association.

D. Liens resulting from judgments against the association are governed by section 33-1256.

33-1252. Conveyance or encumbrance of common elements

A. Portions of the common elements may be conveyed or subjected to a mortgage, deed of trust or security interest by the association if persons entitled to cast at least eighty per cent of the votes in the association, or any larger percentage the declaration specifies, agree to that action in the manner prescribed in subsection B, except that all the owners of units to which any limited common element is allocated must agree in order to convey that limited common element or subject it to a mortgage, deed of trust or security interest. The declaration may specify a smaller percentage only if all of the units in the condominium are restricted exclusively to nonresidential uses. Proceeds of the sale or encumbrance of the common elements are an asset of the association.

B. An agreement to convey common elements or subject them to a mortgage, deed of trust or security interest shall be evidenced by the execution of an agreement, or ratifications of the agreement, in the same manner as a deed, by the requisite number of unit owners. The agreement shall specify a date after which the agreement will be void unless previously recorded. The agreement and all ratifications of the agreement shall be recorded in each county in which a portion of the condominium is situated and are effective only on recordation.

C. The association, on behalf of the unit owners, may contract to convey common elements or subject them to a mortgage, deed of trust or security interest, but the contract is not enforceable against the association until approved pursuant to subsections A and B. Thereafter, the association has all powers necessary and appropriate to effect the conveyance or encumbrance, including the power to execute deeds or other instruments.

D. Except as permitted in this chapter, any purported conveyance, encumbrance, judicial sale or other voluntary transfer of common elements is void.

E. A conveyance or encumbrance of common elements pursuant to this section does not deprive any unit of its rights of access and support.

F. A conveyance or encumbrance of common elements pursuant to this section does not affect the priority or validity of preexisting encumbrances.

33-1253. Insurance

A. Commencing not later than the time of the first conveyance of a unit to a person other than a declarant, the association shall maintain, to the extent reasonably available, both:

    1. Property insurance on the common elements insuring against all risks of direct physical loss commonly insured against or, as determined by the board of directors against fire and extended coverage perils. The total amount of insurance after application of any deductibles shall be not less than eighty per cent of the actual cash value of the insured property at the time the insurance is purchased and at each renewal date, exclusive of land, excavations, foundations and other items normally excluded from property policies.

    2. Liability insurance in an amount determined by the board of directors but not less than any amount specified in the declaration, covering all occurrences commonly insured against for death, bodily injury and property damage arising out of or in connection with the use, ownership or maintenance of the common elements.

B. To the extent available, the insurance maintained under subsection A, paragraph 1 of this section, if determined by the board, includes the units or any portion of those units but need not include improvements and betterments installed by unit owners or the personal property of unit owners.

C. If the insurance described in subsection A of this section is not reasonably available, the association promptly shall cause notice of that fact to be hand-delivered or sent prepaid by United States mail to all unit owners. The declaration may require the association to carry any other insurance, and the association in any event may carry any other insurance it deems appropriate to protect the association or the unit owners.

D. Insurance policies carried pursuant to subsection A of this section shall provide the following:

    1. Each unit owner is an insured person under the policy with respect to liability arising out of his interest in the common elements or membership in the association.

    2. The insurer waives its right to subrogation under the policy against any unit owner or members of his household.

    3. No act or omission by any unit owner, unless acting within the scope of his authority on behalf of the association, will void the policy or be a condition to recovery under the policy.

    4. If, at the time of a loss under the policy, there is other insurance in the name of a unit owner covering the same property covered by the policy, the association's policy provides primary insurance.

E. Any loss covered by the property policy under subsection A, paragraph 1 and subsection B of this section shall be adjusted with the association, but the insurance proceeds for that loss are payable to any insurance trustee designated for that purpose, or otherwise to the association, and not to any mortgagee or beneficiary under a deed of trust. The insurance trustee or the association shall hold any insurance proceeds in trust for unit owners and lienholders as their interests may appear. Subject to the provisions of subsection H of this section, the proceeds shall be disbursed first for the repair or restoration of the damaged property, and unit owners and lienholders are not entitled to receive payment of any portion of the proceeds unless there is a surplus of proceeds after the property has been completely repaired or restored, or the condominium is terminated.

F. An insurance policy issued to the association does not prevent a unit owner from obtaining insurance for his own benefit.

G. An insurer that has issued an insurance policy under this section shall issue certificates or memoranda of insurance to the association and, on written request, to any unit owner, mortgagee or beneficiary under a deed of trust. The insurer issuing the policy shall not cancel or refuse to renew it until thirty days after notice of the proposed cancellation or nonrenewal has been mailed to the association, each unit owner and each mortgagee or beneficiary under a deed of trust to whom a certificate or memorandum of insurance has been issued at their respective last known addresses.

H. Any portion of the condominium for which insurance is required under this section which is damaged or destroyed shall be repaired or replaced promptly by the association unless any of the following apply:

1. The condominium is terminated.

2. Repair or replacement would be illegal under any state or local health or safety statute or ordinance.

3. Eighty per cent of the unit owners, including every owner of a unit or allocated limited common element, which will not be rebuilt, vote not to rebuild.

I. The cost of repair or replacement in excess of insurance proceeds and reserves is a common expense. If the entire condominium is not repaired or replaced:

1. The insurance proceeds attributable to the damaged common elements in proportion to their common element interests or as otherwise provided in the declaration shall be used to restore the damaged area to a condition compatible with the remainder of the condominium.

2. The insurance proceeds attributable to units and allocated limited common elements which are not rebuilt shall be distributed in proportion to their common element interests or as otherwise provided in the declaration to the owners of those units and the owners of the units to which those limited common elements were allocated, or to lienholders as their interests may appear.

3. The remainder of the proceeds shall be distributed to all the unit owners or lienholders as their interests may appear in proportion to the common element interests of all the units.

J. If the unit owners vote not to rebuild any unit, that unit's allocated interests are automatically reallocated on the vote as if the unit had been condemned under section 33-1206, subsection A, and the association promptly shall prepare, execute and record an amendment to the declaration reflecting the reallocations.

K. Notwithstanding the provisions of subsections H, I and J of this section, section 33-1228 governs the distribution of insurance proceeds if the condominium is terminated.

L. If all units are restricted to nonresidential use, the provisions of a subsection or paragraph of this section do not apply if the declaration, articles of incorporation or amended bylaws contain provisions inconsistent with such subsection or paragraph.

M. This section does not prohibit the declaration from requiring additional or greater amounts of insurance coverage or does not prohibit the board of directors from acquiring additional or greater amounts of coverage as it reasonably deems appropriate.

33-1254. Surplus monies

Unless otherwise provided in the declaration, any surplus monies of the association remaining after payment of or provision for common expenses and any prepayment of reserves shall be paid to the unit owners in proportion to their common expense liabilities or credited to them to reduce their future common expense assessments.

33-1255. Assessments for common expenses; applicability

A. Until the association makes a common expense assessment, the declarant shall pay all common expenses. After any assessment has been made by the association, assessments shall be made at least annually, based on a budget adopted at least annually by the association.

B. Except for assessments under subsections C, D, E and F of this section, all common expenses shall be assessed against all the units in accordance with the allocations set forth in the declaration pursuant to section 33-1217, subsection A. Any past due common expense assessment or installment bears interest at the rate established by the board subject to the condominium documents.

C. Unless otherwise provided for in the declaration all of the following apply:

1. Any common expense associated with the maintenance, repair or replacement of a limited common element shall be equally assessed against the units to which the limited common element is assigned.

2. Any common expense or portion of a common expense benefitting fewer than all of the units shall be assessed exclusively against the units benefitted.

D. Assessments to pay a judgment against the association may be made only against the units in the condominium at the time the judgment was entered, in proportion to their common expense liabilities.

E. If any common expense is caused by the misconduct of any unit owner, the association may assess that expense exclusively against that unit.

F. If the declaration so provides, the common expense assessment for any unit on which construction has not been substantially completed may be an amount which is not less than twenty-five per cent of the common expense assessment for units which have been substantially completed. However, this reduced common expense assessment shall not be permitted, unless the declarant is obligated under the declaration to pay to the association any deficiency in monies due to the declarant having paid a reduced common assessment and necessary for the association to be able to timely pay all common expenses.

G. If common expense liabilities are reallocated, common expense assessments and any installment on the assessments not yet due shall be recalculated in accordance with the reallocated common expense liabilities.

H. This section does not apply to timeshare plans or associations that are subject to chapter 20 of this title.

33-1256. Lien for assessments; priority; mechanics' and materialmen's liens; applicability

A. The association has a lien on a unit for any assessment levied against that unit from the time the assessment becomes due. The association's lien for assessments, for charges for late payment of those assessments, for reasonable collection fees and for reasonable attorney fees and costs incurred with respect to those assessments may be foreclosed in the same manner as a mortgage on real estate but may be foreclosed only if the owner has been delinquent in the payment of monies secured by the lien, excluding reasonable collection fees, reasonable attorney fees and charges for late payment of and costs incurred with respect to those assessments, for a period of one year or in the amount of one thousand two hundred dollars or more, whichever occurs first. Fees, charges, late charges, monetary penalties and interest charged pursuant to section 33-1242, subsection A, paragraphs 10, 11 and 12, other than charges for late payment of assessments, are not enforceable as assessments under this section. If an assessment is payable in installments, the full amount of the assessment is a lien from the time the first installment of the assessment becomes due. The association has a lien for fees, charges, late charges, other than charges for late payment of assessments, monetary penalties or interest charged pursuant to section 33-1242, subsection A, paragraphs 10, 11 and 12 after the entry of a judgment in a civil suit for those fees, charges, late charges, monetary penalties or interest from a court of competent jurisdiction and the recording of that judgment in the office of the county recorder as otherwise provided by law. The association's lien for monies other than for assessments, for charges for late payment of those assessments, for reasonable collection fees and for reasonable attorney fees and costs incurred with respect to those assessments may not be foreclosed and is effective only on conveyance of any interest in the real property.

B. A lien for assessments, for charges for late payment of those assessments, for reasonable collection fees and for reasonable attorney fees and costs incurred with respect to those assessments under this section is prior to all other liens, interests and encumbrances on a unit except:

1. Liens and encumbrances recorded before the recordation of the declaration.

2. A recorded first mortgage on the unit, a seller's interest in a first contract for sale pursuant to chapter 6, article 3 of this title on the unit recorded prior to the lien arising pursuant to subsection A of this section or a recorded first deed of trust on the unit.

3. Liens for real estate taxes and other governmental assessments or charges against the unit.

C. Subsection B of this section does not affect the priority of mechanics' or materialmen's liens or the priority of liens for other assessments made by the association. The lien under this section is not subject to chapter 8 of this title.

D. Unless the declaration otherwise provides, if two or more associations have liens for assessments created at any time on the same real estate, those liens have equal priority.

E. Recording of the declaration constitutes record notice and perfection of the lien for assessments, for charges for late payment of those assessments, for reasonable collection fees and for reasonable attorney fees and costs incurred with respect to those assessments. Further recordation of any claim of lien for assessments under this section is not required.

F. A lien for unpaid assessments is extinguished unless proceedings to enforce the lien are instituted within three years after the full amount of the assessments becomes due.

G. This section does not prohibit actions to recover sums for which subsection A of this section creates a lien or does not prohibit an association from taking a deed in lieu of foreclosure.

H. A judgment or decree in any action brought under this section shall include costs and reasonable attorney fees for the prevailing party.

I. The association on written request shall furnish to a lienholder, escrow agent, unit owner or person designated by a unit owner a statement setting forth the amount of unpaid assessments against the unit. The statement shall be furnished within ten days after receipt of the request and the statement is binding on the association, the board of directors and every unit owner if the statement is requested by an escrow agency that is licensed pursuant to title 6, chapter 7. Failure to provide the statement to the escrow agent within the time provided for in this subsection shall extinguish any lien for any unpaid assessment then due.

J. The association shall record in the office of the county recorder in the county in which the condominium is located a notice stating the name of the association or designated agent or management company for the association, the address for the association and the telephone number of the association or its designated agent or management company. The notice shall include the name of the condominium community, the date of the recording and the recorded instrument number or book and page for the main document that constitutes the declaration. If an association's address, designated agent or management company changes, the association shall amend its notice or record a new notice within ninety days after the change.

K. Notwithstanding any provision in the condominium documents or in any contract between the association and a management company, unless the member directs otherwise, all payments received on a member's account shall be applied first to any unpaid assessments, for unpaid charges for late payment of those assessments, for reasonable collection fees and for unpaid attorney fees and costs incurred with respect to those assessments, in that order, with any remaining amounts applied next to other unpaid fees, charges and monetary penalties or interest and late charges on any of those amounts.

L. This section does not apply to timeshare plans or associations that are subject to chapter 20 of this title.

33-1257. Other liens affecting the condominium

A. Except as provided in subsection B of this section, a legally recorded judgment for money against the association is not a lien on the common elements but is a lien in favor of the judgment lienholder against all of the units in the condominium at the time the judgment was entered. Other property of a unit owner is not subject to the claims of creditors of the association.

B. If the association has granted a mortgage, deed of trust or security interest in the common elements to a creditor of the association pursuant to section 33-1252, the holder of that security interest must exercise its right against the common elements before its judgment lien on any unit may be enforced.

C. Whether perfected before or after the creation of the condominium, if a lien other than a deed of trust or mortgage becomes effective against two or more units, the unit owner of an affected unit may pay to the lienholder the amount of the lien attributable to his unit, and the lienholder, on receipt of payment, shall promptly deliver a release of the lien covering that unit. The amount of the payment shall be proportionate to the ratio which that unit owner's common expense liability bears to the common expense liabilities of all unit owners whose units are subject to the lien. After payment, the association shall not assess or have a lien against that unit owner's unit for any portion of the common expenses incurred in connection with that lien.

D. A judgment against the association shall be indexed in the name of the condominium and the association and shall include the legal description of the unit subject to the lien. When so indexed, the judgment is notice of the lien against the units.

33-1258. Association financial and other records; applicability

A. Except as provided in subsection B of this section, all financial and other records of the association shall be made reasonably available for examination by any member or any person designated by the member in writing as the member's representative. The association shall not charge a member or any person designated by the member in writing for making material available for review. The association shall have ten business days to fulfill a request for examination. On request for purchase of copies of records by any member or any person designated by the member in writing as the member's representative, the association shall have ten business days to provide copies of the requested records. An association may charge a fee for making copies of not more than fifteen cents per page.

B. Books and records kept by or on behalf of the association and the board may be withheld from disclosure to the extent that the portion withheld relates to any of the following:

1. Privileged communication between an attorney for the association and the association.

2. Pending litigation.

3. Meeting minutes or other records of a session of a board meeting that is not required to be open to all members pursuant to section 33-1248.

4. Personal, health or financial records of an individual member of the association, an individual employee of the association or an individual employee of a contractor for the association, including records of the association directly related to the personal, health or financial information about an individual member of the association, an individual employee of the association or an individual employee of a contractor for the association.

5. Records relating to the job performance of, compensation of, health records of or specific complaints against an individual employee of the association or an individual employee of a contractor of the association who works under the direction of the association.

C. The association shall not be required to disclose financial and other records of the association if disclosure would violate any state or federal law.

D. This section does not apply to an association for a timeshare plan that is subject to chapter 20 of this title.

33-1259. Association as trustee

With respect to a third person dealing with the association in the association's capacity as a trustee, the existence of trust powers and their proper exercise by the association may be assumed without inquiry. A third person is not bound to inquire whether the association has power to act as trustee or is properly exercising trust powers. A third person, without actual knowledge that the association is exceeding or improperly exercising its powers, is fully protected in dealing with the association as if it possessed and properly exercised the powers it purports to exercise. A third person is not bound to assure the proper application of trust assets paid or delivered to the association in its capacity as trustee.

33-1260. Resale of units; information required; fees; civil penalty; applicability; definition

A. For condominiums with fewer than fifty units, a unit owner shall mail or deliver to a purchaser or a purchaser's authorized agent within ten days after receipt of a written notice of a pending sale of the unit, and for condominiums with fifty or more units, the association shall mail or deliver to a purchaser or a purchaser's authorized agent within ten days after receipt of a written notice of a pending sale that contains the name and address of the purchaser, all of the following in either paper or electronic format:

1. A copy of the bylaws and the rules of the association.

2. A copy of the declaration.

3. A dated statement containing:

   a) The telephone number and address of a principal contact for the association, which may be an association manager, an association management company, an officer of the association or any other person designated by the board of directors.

b) The amount of the common expense assessment for the unit and any unpaid common expense assessment, special assessment or other assessment, fee or charge currently due and payable from the selling unit owner. If the request is made by a lienholder, escrow agent, unit owner or person designated by a unit owner pursuant to section 33-1256, failure to provide the information pursuant to this subdivision within the time provided for in this subsection shall extinguish any lien for any unpaid assessment then due against that unit.

c) A statement as to whether a portion of the unit is covered by insurance maintained by the association.

d) The total amount of money held by the association as reserves.

e) If the statement is being furnished by the association, a statement as to whether the records of the association reflect any alterations or improvements to the unit that violate the declaration. The association is not obligated to provide information regarding alterations or improvements that occurred more than six years before the proposed sale. Nothing in this subdivision relieves the seller of a unit from the obligation to disclose alterations or improvements to the unit that violate the declaration, nor precludes the association from taking action against the purchaser of a unit for violations that are apparent at the time of purchase and that are not reflected in the association's records.

f) If the statement is being furnished by the unit owner, a statement as to whether the unit owner has any knowledge of any alterations or improvements to the unit that violate the declaration.

g) A statement of case names and case numbers for pending litigation with respect to the unit filed by the association against the unit owner or filed by the unit owner against the association. The unit owner or the association shall not be required to disclose information concerning the pending litigation that would violate any applicable rule of attorney-client privilege under Arizona law.

h) A statement that provides " I hereby acknowledge that the declaration, bylaws and rules of the association constitute a contract between the association and me (the purchaser). By signing this statement, I acknowledge that I have read and understand the association's contract with me (the purchaser). I also understand that as a matter of Arizona law, if I fail to pay my association assessments, the association may foreclose on my property." The statement shall also include a signature line for the purchaser and shall be returned to the association within fourteen calendar days.

4. A copy of the current operating budget of the association.

5. A copy of the most recent annual financial report of the association. If the report is more than ten pages, the association may provide a summary of the report in lieu of the entire report.

6. A copy of the most recent reserve study of the association, if any.

7. A statement summarizing any pending lawsuits, except those relating to the collection of assessments owed by unit owners other than the selling unit owner, in which the association is a named party, including the amount of any money claimed.

B. A purchaser or seller who is damaged by the failure of the unit owner or the association to disclose the information required by subsection A of this section may pursue all remedies at law or in equity against the unit owner or the association, whichever failed to comply with subsection A of this section, including the recovery of reasonable attorney fees.

C. The association may charge the unit owner a fee of no more than an aggregate of four hundred dollars to compensate the association for the costs incurred in the preparation of a statement or other documents furnished by the association pursuant to this section for purposes of resale disclosure, lien estoppel and any other services related to the transfer or use of the property. In addition, the association may charge a rush fee of no more than one hundred dollars if the rush services are required to be performed within seventy-two hours after the request for rush services, and may charge a statement or other documents update fee of no more than fifty dollars if thirty days or more have passed since the date of the original disclosure statement or the date the documents were delivered. The association shall make available to any interested party the amount of any fee established from time to time by the association. If the aggregate fee for purposes of resale disclosure, lien estoppel and any other services related to the transfer or use of a property is less than four hundred dollars on January 1, 2010, the fee may increase at a rate of no more than twenty per cent per year based on the immediately preceding fiscal year's amount not to exceed the four hundred dollar aggregate fee. The association may charge the same fee without regard to whether the association is furnishing the statement or other documents in paper or electronic format.

D. The fees prescribed by this section shall be collected no earlier than at the close of escrow and may only be charged once to a unit owner for that transaction between the parties specified in the notice required pursuant to subsection A of this section. An association shall not charge or collect a fee relating to services for resale disclosure, lien estoppel and any other services related to the transfer or use of a property except as specifically authorized in this section. An association that charges or collects a fee in violation of this section is subject to a civil penalty of no more than one thousand two hundred dollars.

E. This section applies to a managing agent for an association that is acting on behalf of the association.

F. A sale in which a public report is issued pursuant to sections 32-2183 and 32-2197.02 or a sale pursuant to section 32-2181.02 is exempt from this section.

G. This section does not apply to timeshare plans or associations that are subject to chapter 20 of this title.

H. For the purposes of this section, unless the context otherwise requires, " unit owner" means the seller of the condominium unit title and excludes any real estate salesperson or real estate broker who is licensed under title 32, chapter 20 and who is acting as a salesperson or broker, any escrow agent who is licensed under title 6, chapter 7 and who is acting as an escrow agent and also excludes a trustee of a deed of trust who is selling the property in a trustee's sale pursuant to chapter 6.1 of this title.

33-1260.01. Rental property; unit owner and agent; fee; disclosure

A. A unit owner may use the unit owner's unit as a rental property unless prohibited in the declaration and shall use it in accordance with the declaration's rental time period restrictions.

B. A unit owner may designate in writing a third party to act as the unit owner's agent with respect to all association matters relating to the rental unit. The unit owner shall sign the written designation and shall provide a copy of the written designation to the association. On delivery of the written designation, the association is authorized to conduct all association business relating to the unit owner's rental unit through the designated agent. Any notice given by the association to a unit owner's designated agent on any matter relating to the unit owner's rental unit constitutes notice to the unit owner.

C. Notwithstanding any provision in the condominium documents, on rental of a unit an association shall not require a unit owner or a unit owner's agent to disclose any information regarding a tenant other than the name and contact information for any adults occupying the unit, the time period of the lease, including the beginning and ending dates of the tenancy, and a description and the license plate numbers of the tenants' vehicles. If the condominium is an age restricted condominium, the unit owner, the unit owner's agent or the tenant shall show a government issued identification that bears a photograph and that confirms that the tenant meets the condominium's age restrictions or requirements.

D. On request of an association or its managing agent for the disclosures prescribed in subsection C of this section, the association or its managing agent may charge a fee of not more than twenty-five dollars which shall be paid within fifteen days after the postmarked request. The fee may be charged for each new tenancy for that unit but may not be charged for a renewal of a lease. Except for the fee permitted by this subsection, the association or its managing agent shall not assess, levy or charge a fee or fine or otherwise impose a requirement on a unit owner's rental unit any differently than on an owner-occupied unit in the association.

E. Notwithstanding any provision in the condominium documents, the association is prohibited from doing any of the following:

1. Requiring a unit owner to provide the association with a copy of the tenant's rental application, credit report, lease agreement or rental contract or other personal information except as prescribed by this section. This paragraph does not prohibit the association from acquiring a credit report on a person in an attempt to collect a debt.

2. Requiring the tenant to sign a waiver or other document limiting the tenant's due process rights as a condition of the tenant's occupancy of the rental unit.

3. Prohibiting or otherwise restricting a unit owner from serving on the board of directors based on the owner's not being an occupant of the unit.

4. Imposing on a unit owner or managing agent any fee, assessment, penalty or 33-1261. Flag display; for sale, rent or lease signs; political signs and activities; applicability

F. Any attempt by an association to exceed the fee, assessment, penalty or other charge authorized by subsection D or E of this section voids the fee, assessment, penalty or other charge authorized by subsection D or E of this section. This section does not prevent an association from complying with the housing for older person act of 1995 (P.L. 104-76; 109 Stat. 787).

G. An owner may use a crime free addendum as part of a lease agreement. This section does not prohibit the owner's use of a crime free addendum.

H. This section does not prohibit and an association may lawfully enforce a provision in the condominium documents that restricts the residency of persons who are required to be registered pursuant to section 13-3821 and who are classified as level two or level three offenders.

I. An owner of rental property shall abate criminal activity as authorized in section12-991.

33-1261. Flag display; for sale, rent or lease signs; political signs and activities; applicability

A. Notwithstanding any provision in the condominium documents, an association shall not prohibit the outdoor display of any of the following:

1. The American flag or an official or replica of a flag of the United States army, navy, air force, marine corps or coast guard by a unit owner on that unit owner's property if the American flag or military flag is displayed in a manner consistent with the federal flag code (P.L. 94-344; 90 Stat. 810; 4 United States Code sections 4 through 10).

2. The POW/MIA flag.

3. The Arizona state flag.

4. An Arizona Indian nations flag.

5. The Gadsden flag.

B. The association shall adopt reasonable rules and regulations regarding the placement and manner of display of the American flag, the military flag, the POW/MIA flag, the Arizona state flag or an Arizona Indian nations flag. The association rules may regulate the location and size of flagpoles but shall not prohibit the installation of a flagpole.

C. Notwithstanding any provision in the condominium documents, an association shall not prohibit or charge a fee for the use of, the placement of or the indoor or outdoor display of a for sale, for rent or for lease sign and a sign rider by a unit owner on that owner's property in any combination, including a sign that indicates the unit owner is offering the property for sale by owner. The size of a sign offering a property for sale, for rent or for lease shall be in conformance with the industry standard size sign, which shall not exceed eighteen by twenty-four inches, and the industry standard size sign rider, which shall not exceed six by twenty-four inches. This subsection applies only to a commercially produced sign and an association may prohibit the use of signs that are not commercially produced. With respect to real estate for sale, for rent or for lease in the condominium, an association shall not prohibit in any way other than as is specifically authorized by this section or otherwise regulate any of the following:

1. Temporary open house signs or a unit owner's for sale sign. The association shall not require the use of particular signs indicating an open house or real property for sale and may not further regulate the use of temporary open house or for sale signs that are industry standard size and that are owned or used by the seller or the seller's agent.

2. Open house hours. The association may not limit the hours for an open house for real estate that is for sale in the condominium, except that the association may prohibit an open house being held before 8:00 a.m. or after 6:00 p.m. and may prohibit open house signs on the common elements of the condominium.

3. An owner's or an owner's agent's for rent or for lease sign unless an association's documents prohibit or restrict leasing of a unit or units. An association shall not further regulate a for rent or for lease sign or require the use of a particular for rent or for lease sign other than the for rent or for lease sign shall not be any larger than the industry standard size sign of eighteen by twenty-four inches and on or in the unit owner's property. If rental or leasing of a unit is allowed, the association may prohibit an open house for rental or leasing being held before 8:00 a.m. or after 6:00 p.m.

D. Notwithstanding any provision in the condominium documents, an association shall not prohibit door to door political activity, including solicitations of support or opposition regarding candidates or ballot issues, and shall not prohibit the circulation of political petitions, including candidate nomination petitions or petitions in support of or opposition to an initiative, referendum or recall or other political issue on property normally open to visitors within the association, except that an association may do the following:

1. Restrict or prohibit door-to-door political activity regarding candidates or ballot issues from sunset to sunrise.

2. Require the prominent display of an identification tag for each person engaged in the activity, along with the prominent identification of the candidate or ballot issue that is the subject of the support or opposition.

E. Notwithstanding any provision in the condominium documents, an association shall not prohibit the indoor or outdoor display of a political sign by a unit owner by placement of a sign in the common element ground that is adjacent to the unit or on that unit owner's property, including any limited common elements for that unit, except that an association may prohibit the display of political signs earlier than seventy-one days before the day of an election and later than three days after an election day. An association may regulate the size and number of political signs

103

that may be placed in the common element ground, on a unit owner's property or on a limited common element for that unit if the association's regulation is no more restrictive than any applicable city, town or county ordinance that regulates the size and number of political signs on residential property. If the city, town or county in which the property is located does not regulate the size and number of political signs on residential property, the association shall not limit the number of political signs, except that the maximum aggregate total dimensions of all political signs on a unit owner's property shall not exceed nine square feet. An association shall not make any regulations regarding the number of candidates supported, the number of public officers supported or opposed in a recall or the number of propositions supported or opposed on a political sign. For the purposes of this subsection, " political sign" means a sign that attempts to influence the outcome of an election, including supporting or opposing the recall of a public officer or supporting or opposing the circulation of a petition for a ballot measure, question or proposition or the recall of a public officer.

F. An association shall not require political signs to be commercially produced or professionally manufactured or prohibit the utilization of both sides of a political sign.

G. A condominium is not required to comply with subsection D of this section if the condominium restricts vehicular or pedestrian access to the condominium. Nothing in this section requires a condominium to make its common elements other than roadways and sidewalks that are normally open to visitors available for the circulation of political petitions to anyone who is not an owner or resident of the community.

H. An association or managing agent that violates subsection C of this section forfeits and extinguishes the lien rights authorized under section 33-1256 against that unit for a period of six consecutive months from the date of the violation.

I. This section does not apply to timeshare plans or associations that are subject to chapter 20 of this title.

DISCLAIMER: *We do not warrant or guarantee the completeness of this information. To satisfy yourself as to the accuracy of these statutes you need to do your own checking as Statutes do change from time to time, and although at the time of this writing, the most* *current publication was used, we acknowledge some elements will change from time to time.*

SECTION VII
PLANNED COMMUNITY STATUTES

Communication leads to community, that is, to understanding, intimacy and mutual valuing.

~ Rollo May (1909-1994)
American Psychologist

CHAPTER 16:
PLANNED COMMUNITY STATUTES

ARTICLE 1 GENERAL PROVISIONS

§ **33-1809** Parking; public service and public safety emergency vehicles; definition

§ **33-1810** Board of directors; annual audit

§ **33-1811** Board of directors; contracts; conflict

§ **33-1812** Proxies; absentee ballots; definition

§ **33-1813** Removal of board member; special meeting

§ **33-1814** Slum property; professional management

§ **33-1815** Association authority; commercial signage

§ **33-1816** Solar energy devices; reasonable restrictions; fees and costs

§ **33-1817** Declaration amendment; design, architectural committees; review

§ **33-1818** Community authority over public roadways; applicability

§ 33-1801. Applicability; exemption

A. This chapter applies to all planned communities.

B. Notwithstanding any provisions in the community documents, this chapter does not apply to any school that receives monies from this state, including a charter school, and a school is exempt from regulation or any enforcement action by any homeowners' association that is subject to this chapter. With the exception of homeschools as defined in section 15-802, schools shall not be established within the living units of a homeowners' association. The homeowners' association may enter into a contractual agreement with a school district or charter school to allow use of the homeowners' association's common areas by the school district or charter school.

C. This chapter does not apply to timeshare plans or associations that are subject to chapter 20

33-1802. Definitions

In this chapter and in the community documents, unless the context otherwise requires:

1. "Association" means a nonprofit corporation or unincorporated association of owners that is created pursuant to a declaration to own and operate portions of a planned community and that has the power under the declaration to assess association members to pay the costs and expenses incurred in the performance of the association's obligations under the declaration.

2. "Community documents" means the declaration, bylaws, articles of incorporation, if any, and rules, if any.

   "Declaration" means any instruments, however denominated, that establish a planned community and any amendment to those instruments.

3. "Planned community" means a real estate development that includes real estate owned and operated by or real estate on which an easement to maintain roadways or a covenant to maintain roadways is held by a nonprofit corporation or unincorporated association of owners, that is created for the purpose of managing, maintaining or improving the property and in which the owners of separately owned lots, parcels or units are mandatory members and are required to pay assessments to the association for these purposes. Planned community does not include a timeshare plan or a timeshare association that is governed by chapter 20 of this title or a condominium that is governed by chapter 9 of this title.

33-1803. Penalties; notice to member of violation

A. Unless limitations in the community documents would result in a lower limit for the assessment, the association shall not impose a regular assessment that is more than twenty per cent greater than the immediately preceding fiscal year's assessment without the approval of the majority of the members of the association. Unless reserved to the members of the association, the board of directors may impose reasonable charges for the late payment of assessments. A payment by a member is deemed late if it is unpaid fifteen or more days after its due date, unless the community documents provide for a longer period. Charges for the late payment of assessments are limited to the greater of fifteen dollars or ten per cent of the amount of the unpaid assessment. Any monies paid by the member for an unpaid assessment shall be applied first to the principal amount unpaid and then to the interest accrued.

B. After notice and an opportunity to be heard, the board of directors may impose reasonable monetary penalties on members for violations of the declaration, bylaws and rules of the association. Notwithstanding any provision in the community documents, the board of directors shall not impose a charge for a late payment of a penalty that exceeds the greater of fifteen dollars or ten per cent of the amount of the unpaid penalty. A payment is deemed late if it is unpaid fifteen or more days after its due date, unless the declaration, bylaws or rules of the association provide for a longer period. Any monies paid by a member for an unpaid penalty shall be applied first to the principal amount unpaid and then to the interest accrued. Notice pursuant to this subsection shall include information pertaining to the manner in which the penalty shall be enforced.

C. A member who receives a written notice that the condition of the property owned by the member is in violation of the community documents without regard to whether a monetary penalty is imposed by the notice may provide the association with a written response by sending the response by certified mail within ten business days after the date of the notice. The response shall be sent to the address contained in the notice or in the recorded notice prescribed by section 33-1807, subsection J.

D. Within ten business days after receipt of the certified mail containing the response from the member, the association shall respond to the member with a written explanation regarding the notice that shall provide at least the following information unless previously provided in the notice of violation:

1. The provision of the community documents that has allegedly been violated.

2. The date of the violation or the date the violation was observed.

3. The first and last name of the person or persons who observed the violation.

4. The process the member must follow to contest the notice.

E. Unless the information required in subsection D, paragraph 4 of this section is provided in the notice of violation, the association shall not proceed with any action to enforce the community documents, including the collection of attorney fees, before or during the time prescribed by subsection D of this section regarding the exchange of information between the association and the member. At any time before or after completion of the exchange of information pursuant to this section, the member may petition for a hearing pursuant to section 41-2198.01 if the dispute is within the jurisdiction of the department of fire, building and life safety as prescribed in section 41-2198.01, subsection B.

33-1804. Open meetings; exceptions

A. Notwithstanding any provision in the declaration, bylaws or other documents to the contrary, all meetings of the members' association and the board of directors, and any regularly scheduled committee meetings, are open to all members of the association or any person designated by a member in writing as the member's representative and all members or designated representatives so desiring shall be permitted to attend and speak at an appropriate time during the deliberations and proceedings. The board may place reasonable time restrictions on those persons speaking during the meeting but shall permit a member or member's designated representative to speak once after the board has discussed a specific agenda item but before the board takes formal action on that item in addition to any other opportunities to speak. The board shall provide for a reasonable number of persons to speak on each side of an issue. Persons attending may tape record or videotape those portions of the meetings of the board of directors and meetings of the members that are open. The board of directors of the association may adopt reasonable rules governing the taping of open portions of the meetings of the board and the membership, but such rules shall not preclude such tape recording or videotaping by those attending. Any portion of a meeting may be closed only if that closed portion of the meeting is limited to consideration of one or more of the following:

1. Legal advice from an attorney for the board or the association. On final resolution of any matter for which the board received legal advice or that concerned pending or contemplated

111

litigation, the board may disclose information about that matter in an open meeting except for matters that are required to remain confidential by the terms of a settlement agreement or judgment.

2. Pending or contemplated litigation.

3. Personal, health or financial information about an individual member of the association, an individual employee of the association or an individual employee of a contractor for the association, including records of the association directly related to the personal, health or financial information about an individual member of the association, an individual employee of the association or an individual employee of a contractor for the association.

4. Matters relating to the job performance of, compensation of, health records of or specific complaints against an individual employee of the association or an individual employee of a contractor of the association who works under the direction of the association.

5. Discussion of a member's appeal of any violation cited or penalty imposed by the association except on request of the affected member that the meeting be held in an open session.

B. Notwithstanding any provision in the community documents, all meetings of the members' association and the board shall be held in this state. A meeting of the members' association shall be held at least once each year. Special meetings of the members' association may be called by the president, by a majority of the board of directors or by members having at least twenty-five per cent, or any lower percentage specified in the bylaws, of the votes in the association. Not fewer than ten nor more than fifty days in advance of any meeting of the members the secretary shall cause notice to be hand-delivered or sent prepaid by United States mail to the mailing address for each lot, parcel or unit owner or to any other mailing address designated in writing by a member. The notice shall state the time and place of the meeting. A notice of any special meeting of the members shall also state the purpose for which the meeting is called, including the general nature of any proposed amendment to the declaration or bylaws, changes in assessments that require approval of the members and any proposal to remove a director or an officer. The failure of any member to receive actual notice of a meeting of the members does not affect the validity of any action taken at that meeting.

C. Notwithstanding any provision in the declaration, bylaws or other community documents, for meetings of the board of directors that are held after the termination of declarant control of the association, notice to members of meetings of the board of directors shall be given at least forty-eight hours in advance of the meeting by newsletter, conspicuous posting or any other reasonable means as determined by the board of directors. An affidavit of notice by an officer of the corporation is prima facie evidence that notice was given as prescribed by this section. Notice to members of meetings of the board of directors is not required if emergency circumstances require action by the board before notice can be given. Any notice of a board meeting shall state the time and place of the meeting. The failure of any member to receive actual notice of a meeting of the board of directors does not affect the validity of any action taken at that meeting.

D. Notwithstanding any provision in the declaration, bylaws or other community documents, for meetings of the board of directors that are held after the termination of declarant control of the association, all of the following apply:

1. The agenda shall be available to all members attending.

2. An emergency meeting of the board of directors may be called to discuss business or take action that cannot be delayed until the next regularly scheduled board meeting. The minutes of the emergency meeting shall state the reason necessitating the emergency meeting. The minutes of the emergency meeting shall be read and approved at the next regularly scheduled meeting of the board of directors.

3. A quorum of the board of directors may meet by means of a telephone conference if a speakerphone is available in the meeting room that allows board members and association members to hear all parties who are speaking during the meeting.

4. Any quorum of the board of directors that meets informally to discuss association business, including workshops, shall comply with the open meeting and notice provisions of this section without regard to whether the board votes or takes any action on any matter at that informal meeting.

E. It is the policy of this state as reflected in this section that all meetings of a planned community, whether meetings of the members' association or meetings of the board of directors of the association, be conducted openly and that notices and agendas be provided for those meetings that contain the information that is reasonably necessary to inform the members of the matters to be discussed or decided and to ensure that members have the ability to speak after discussion of agenda items, but before a vote of the board of directors is taken. Toward this end, any person or entity that is charged with the interpretation of these provisions shall take into account this declaration of policy and shall construe any provision of this section in favor of open meetings.

33-1805. Association financial and other records

A. Except as provided in subsection B of this section, all financial and other records of the association shall be made reasonably available for examination by any member or any person designated by the member in writing as the member's representative. The association shall not charge a member or any person designated by the member in writing for making material available for review. The association shall have ten business days to fulfill a request for examination. On request for purchase of copies of records by any member or any person designated by the member in writing as the member's representative, the association shall have ten business days to provide copies of the requested records. An association may charge a fee for making copies of not more than fifteen cents per page.

B. Books and records kept by or on behalf of the association and the board may be withheld from disclosure to the extent that the portion withheld relates to any of the following:

  1. Privileged communication between an attorney for the association and the association.

  2. Pending litigation.

  3. Meeting minutes or other records of a session of a board meeting that is not required to be open to all members pursuant to section 33-1804.

  4. Personal, health or financial records of an individual member of the association, an individual employee of the association or an individual employee of a contractor for the association, including records of the association directly related to the

personal, health or financial information about an individual member of the association, an individual employee of the association or an individual employee of a contractor for the association.

5. Records relating to the job performance of, compensation of, health records of or specific complaints against an individual employee of the association or an individual employee of a contractor of the association who works under the direction of the association.

C. The association shall not be required to disclose financial and other records of the association if disclosure would violate any state or federal law.

33-1806. Resale of units; information required; fees; civil penalty; definition

A. For planned communities with fewer than fifty units, a member shall mail or deliver to a purchaser or a purchaser's authorized agent within ten days after receipt of a written notice of a pending sale of the unit, and for planned communities with fifty or more units, the association shall mail or deliver to a purchaser or a purchaser's authorized agent within ten days after receipt of a written notice of a pending sale that contains the name and address of the purchaser, all of the following in either paper or electronic format:

1. A copy of the bylaws and the rules of the association.

2. A copy of the declaration.

3. A dated statement containing:

   a) The telephone number and address of a principal contact for the association, which may be an association manager, an association management company, an officer of the association or any other person designated by the board of directors.

   b) The amount of the common regular assessment and the unpaid common regular assessment, special assessment or other assessment, fee or charge currently due and payable from the selling member. If the request is made by a lienholder, escrow agent, member or person designated by a member pursuant to section 33-1807, failure to provide the information pursuant to this subdivision within the time provided for in this subsection shall extinguish any lien for any unpaid assessment then due against that property.

c) A statement as to whether a portion of the unit is covered by insurance maintained by the association.

d) The total amount of money held by the association as reserves.

e) If the statement is being furnished by the association, a statement as to whether the records of the association reflect any alterations or improvements to the unit that violate the declaration. The association is not obligated to provide information regarding alterations or improvements that occurred more than six years before the proposed sale. Nothing in this subdivision relieves the seller of a unit from the obligation to disclose alterations or improvements to the unit that violate the declaration, nor precludes the association from taking action against the purchaser of a unit for violations that are apparent at the time of purchase and that are not reflected in the association's records.

f) If the statement is being furnished by the member, a statement as to whether the member has any knowledge of any alterations or improvements to the unit that violate the declaration.

g) A statement of case names and case numbers for pending litigation with respect to the unit filed by the association against the member or filed by the member against the association. The member shall not be required to disclose information concerning such pending litigation that would violate any applicable rule of attorney-client privilege under Arizona law.

h) A statement that provides "I hereby acknowledge that the declaration, bylaws and rules of the association constitute a contract between the association and me (the purchaser). By signing this statement, I acknowledge that I have read and understand the association's contract with me (the purchaser). I also understand that as a matter of Arizona law, if I fail to pay my association assessments, the association may foreclose on my property." The statement shall also include a signature line for the purchaser and shall be returned to the association within fourteen calendar days.

4. A copy of the current operating budget of the association.

5. A copy of the most recent annual financial report of the association. If the report is more than ten pages, the association may provide a summary of the report in lieu of the entire report.

6. A copy of the most recent reserve study of the association, if any.

7. A statement summarizing any pending lawsuits, except those relating to the collection of assessments owed by members other than the selling member, in which the association is a named party, including the amount of any money claimed.

B. A purchaser or seller who is damaged by the failure of the member or the association to disclose the information required by subsection A of this section may pursue all remedies at law or in equity against the member or the association, whichever failed to comply with subsection A of this section, including the recovery of reasonable attorney fees.

C. The association may charge the member a fee of no more than an aggregate of four hundred dollars to compensate the association for the costs incurred in the preparation of a statement or other documents furnished by the association pursuant to this section for purposes of resale disclosure, lien estoppel and any other services related to the transfer or use of the property. In addition, the association may charge a rush fee of no more than one hundred dollars if the rush services are required to be performed within seventy-two hours after the request for rush services, and may charge a statement or other documents update fee of no more than fifty dollars if thirty days or more have passed since the date of the original disclosure statement or the date the documents were delivered. The association shall make available to any interested party the amount of any fee established from time to time by the association. If the aggregate fee for purposes of resale disclosure, lien estoppel and any other services related to the transfer or use of a property is less than four hundred dollars on January 1, 2010, the fee may increase at a rate of no more than twenty per cent per year based on the immediately preceding fiscal year's amount not to exceed the four hundred dollar aggregate fee. The association may charge the same fee without regard to whether the association is furnishing the statement or other documents in paper or electronic format.

D. The fees prescribed by this section shall be collected no earlier than at the close of escrow and may only be charged once to a member for that transaction between the parties specified in the notice required pursuant to subsection A of this section. An association shall not charge or collect a fee relating to services for resale disclosure, lien estoppel and any other services related to the transfer or use of a property except as specifically authorized in this section. An association that charges or collects a fee in violation of this section is subject to a civil penalty of no more than one thousand two hundred dollars.

E. This section applies to a managing agent for an association that is acting on behalf of the association.

F. The following are exempt from this section:

1. A sale in which a public report is issued pursuant to sections 32-2183 and 32-2197.02.

2. A sale pursuant to section 32-2181.02.

3. A conveyance by recorded deed that bears an exemption listed in section 11-1134, subsection B, paragraph 3 or 7. On recordation of the deed and for no additional charge, the member shall provide the association with the changes in ownership including the member's name, billing address and phone number. Failure to provide the information shall not prevent the member from qualifying for the exemption pursuant to this section.

G. For the purposes of this section, unless the context otherwise requires, " member" means the seller of the unit title and excludes any real estate salesperson or real estate broker who is licensed under title 32, chapter 20 and who is acting as a salesperson or broker, any escrow agent who is licensed under title 6, chapter 7 and who is acting as an escrow agent and also excludes a trustee of a deed of trust who is selling the property in a trustee's sale pursuant to chapter 6.1 of this title.

33-1806.01. Rental property; member and agent information; fee; disclosure

A. A member may use the member's property as a rental property unless prohibited in the declaration and shall use it in accordance with the declaration's rental time period restrictions.

B. A member may designate in writing a third party to act as the member's agent with respect to all association matters relating to the rental property. The member shall sign the written designation and shall provide a copy of the written designation to the association. On delivery of the written designation, the association is authorized to conduct all association business relating to the member's rental property through the designated agent. Any notice given by the association to a member's designated agent on any matter relating to the member's rental property constitutes notice to the member.

C. Notwithstanding any provision in the community documents, on rental of a member's property an association shall not require a member or a member's agent to disclose any information regarding a tenant other than the name and contact information for any adults occupying the property, the time period of the lease, including the beginning and ending dates of the tenancy, and a description and the license plate numbers of the tenants' vehicles. If the planned community is an age restricted community, the member, the member's agent or the tenant shall show a government issued identification that bears a photograph and that confirms that the tenant meets the community's age restrictions or requirements.

D. On request of an association or its managing agent for the disclosures prescribed in subsection C of this section, the association or its managing agent may charge a fee of not more than twenty-five dollars which shall be paid within fifteen days after the postmarked request. The fee may be charged for each new tenancy for that property but may not be charged for a renewal of a lease. Except for the fee permitted by this subsection, the association or its managing agent shall not assess, levy or charge a fee or fine or otherwise impose a requirement on a member's rental property any differently than on an owner-occupied property in the association.

E. Notwithstanding any provision in the community documents, the association is prohibited from doing any of the following:

1. Requiring a member to provide the association with a copy of the tenant's rental application, credit report, lease agreement or rental contract or other personal information except as prescribed by this section. This paragraph does not prohibit the association from acquiring a credit report on a person in an attempt to collect a debt.

2. Requiring the tenant to sign a waiver or other document limiting the tenant's due process rights as a condition of the tenant's occupancy of the rental property.

3. Prohibiting or otherwise restricting a member from serving on the board of directors based on the member's not being an occupant of the property.

4. Imposing on a member or managing agent any fee, assessment, penalty or other charge in an amount greater than fifteen dollars for incomplete or late information regarding the information requested pursuant to subsection C of this section. Any attempt by an association to charge a fee, assessment, penalty or other charge that is not authorized by this section voids the fee authorized under subsection D of this section and voids the requirement to provide the information to the association that is prescribed in subsection C of this section.

F. Any attempt by an association to exceed the fee, assessment, penalty or other charge authorized by subsection D or E of this section voids the fee, assessment, penalty or other charge authorized by subsection D or E of this section. This section does not prevent an association from complying with the housing for older persons act of 1995 (P.L. 104-76; 109 Stat. 787).

G. An owner may use a crime free addendum as part of a lease agreement. This section does not prohibit the owner's use of a crime free addendum.

H. This section does not prohibit and an association may lawfully enforce a provision in the community documents that restricts the residency of persons who are required to be registered pursuant to section 13-3821 and who are classified as level two or level three offenders.

I. An owner of rental property shall abate criminal activity as authorized in section 12-991.

33-1807. Lien for assessments; priority; mechanics' and materialmen's liens

A. The association has a lien on a unit for any assessment levied against that unit from the time the assessment becomes due. The association's lien for assessments, for charges for late payment of those assessments, for reasonable collection fees and for reasonable attorney fees and costs incurred with respect to those assessments may be foreclosed in the same manner as a mortgage on real estate but may be foreclosed only if the owner has been delinquent in the payment of monies secured by the lien, excluding reasonable collection fees, reasonable attorney fees and charges for late payment of and costs incurred with respect to those assessments, for a period of one year or in the amount of one thousand two hundred dollars or more, whichever occurs first. Fees, charges, late charges, monetary penalties and interest charged pursuant to section 33-1803, other than charges for late payment of assessments are not enforceable as assessments under this section. If an assessment is payable in installments, the full amount of the assessment is a lien from the time the first installment of the assessment becomes due. The association has a lien for fees, charges, late charges, other than charges for late payment of assessments, monetary penalties or interest charged pursuant to section 33-1803 after the entry of a judgment in a civil suit for those fees, charges, late charges, monetary penalties or interest from a court of competent jurisdiction and the recording of that judgment in the office of the county recorder as otherwise provided by law. The association's lien for monies other than for assessments, for charges for late payment of those assessments, for reasonable collection fees and for reasonable attorney fees and costs incurred with respect to those assessments may not be foreclosed and is effective only on conveyance of any interest in the real property.

B. A lien for assessments, for charges for late payment of those assessments, for reasonable collection fees and for reasonable attorney fees and costs incurred with respect to those assessments under this section is prior to all other liens, interests and encumbrances on a unit except:

1. Liens and encumbrances recorded before the recordation of the declaration.

2. A recorded first mortgage on the unit, a seller's interest in a first contract for sale pursuant to chapter 6, article 3 of this

title on the unit recorded prior to the lien arising pursuant to subsection A of this section or a recorded first deed of trust on the unit.

3. Liens for real estate taxes and other governmental assessments or charges against the unit.

C. Subsection B of this section does not affect the priority of mechanics' or materialmen's liens or the priority of liens for other assessments made by the association. The lien under this section is not subject to chapter 8 of this title.

D. Unless the declaration otherwise provides, if two or more associations have liens for assessments created at any time on the same real estate those liens have equal priority.

E. Recording of the declaration constitutes record notice and perfection of the lien for assessments, for charges for late payment of assessments, for reasonable collection fees and for reasonable attorney fees and costs incurred with respect to those assessments. Further recordation of any claim of lien for assessments under this section is not required.

F. A lien for an unpaid assessment is extinguished unless proceedings to enforce the lien are instituted within three years after the full amount of the assessment becomes due.

G. This section does not prohibit:

1. Actions to recover amounts for which subsection A of this section creates a lien.

2. An association from taking a deed in lieu of foreclosure.

H. A judgment or decree in any action brought under this section shall include costs and reasonable attorney fees for the prevailing party.

I. On written request, the association shall furnish to a lienholder, escrow agent, unit owner or person designated by a unit owner a statement setting forth the amount of any unpaid assessment against the unit. The association shall furnish the statement within ten days after receipt of the request, and the statement is binding on the association, the board of directors and every unit owner if the statement is requested by an escrow agency that is licensed pursuant to title 6, chapter 7. Failure to provide the statement to the escrow agent within the time provided for in this subsection shall extinguish any lien for any unpaid assessment then due.

J. Notwithstanding any provision in the community documents or in any contract between the association and a management company, unless the member directs otherwise, all payments received on a member's account shall be applied first to any unpaid assessments, for unpaid charges for late payment of those assessments, for reasonable collection fees and for unpaid attorney fees and costs incurred with respect to those assessments, in that order, with any remaining amounts applied next to other unpaid fees, charges and monetary penalties or interest and late charges on any of those amounts.

33-1808. Flag display; political signs; caution signs; for sale, rent or lease signs; political activities

A. Notwithstanding any provision in the community documents, an association shall not prohibit the outdoor front yard or backyard display of any of the following:

  1. The American flag or an official or replica of a flag of the United States army, navy, air force, marine corps or coast guard by an association member on that member's property if the American flag or military flag is displayed in a manner consistent with the federal flag code (P.L. 94-344; 90 Stat. 810; 4 United States Code sections 4 through 10).

  2. The POW/MIA flag.

  3. The Arizona state flag.

  4. An Arizona Indian nations flag.

  5. The Gadsden flag.

B. The association shall adopt reasonable rules and regulations regarding the placement and manner of display of the American flag, the military flag, the POW/MIA flag, the Arizona state flag or an Arizona Indian nations flag. The association rules may regulate the location and size of flagpoles, may limit the member to displaying no more than two flags at once and may limit the height of the flagpole to no more than the height of the rooftop of the member's home but shall not prohibit the installation of a flagpole in the front yard or backyard of the member's property.

C. Notwithstanding any provision in the community documents, an association shall not prohibit the indoor or outdoor display of a political sign by an association member on that member's property, except that an association may prohibit the display of political signs earlier than seventy-one days before the day of an election and later than three days after an election day. An association may regulate the size and number of political signs that may be placed on a member's property if the association's regulation is no more restrictive than any applicable city, town or county ordinance that regulates the size and number of political signs on residential property. If the city, town or county in which the property is located does not regulate the size and number of political signs on residential property, the association shall not limit the number of political signs, except that the maximum aggregate total dimensions of all political signs on a member's property shall not exceed nine square feet. For the purposes of this subsection, " political sign" means a sign that attempts to influence the outcome of an election, including supporting or opposing the recall of a public officer or supporting or opposing the circulation of a petition for a ballot measure, question or proposition or the recall of a public officer.

D. Notwithstanding any provision in the community documents, an association shall not prohibit the use of cautionary signs regarding children if the signs are used and displayed as follows:

1. The signs are displayed in residential areas only.

2. The signs are removed within one hour of children ceasing to play.

3. The signs are displayed only when children are actually present within fifty feet of the sign.

4. The temporary signs are no taller than three feet in height.

5. The signs are professionally manufactured or produced.

E. Notwithstanding any provision in the community documents, an association shall not prohibit children who reside in the planned community from engaging in recreational activity on residential roadways that are under the jurisdiction of the association and on which the posted speed limit is twenty-five miles per hour or less.

F. Notwithstanding any provision in the community documents, an association shall not prohibit or charge a fee for the use of, placement of or the indoor or outdoor display of a for sale, for rent or for lease sign and a sign rider by an association member on that member's property in any combination, including a sign that indicates the member is offering the property for sale by owner. The size of a sign offering a property for sale, for rent or for lease shall be in conformance with the industry standard size sign, which shall not exceed eighteen by twenty-four inches, and the industry standard size sign rider, which shall not exceed six by twenty-four inches. This subsection applies only to a commercially produced sign, and an association may prohibit the use of signs that are not commercially produced. With respect to real estate for sale, for rent or for lease in the planned community, an association shall not prohibit in any way other than as is specifically authorized by this section or otherwise regulate any of the following:

1. Temporary open house signs or a member's for sale sign. The association shall not require the use of particular signs indicating an open house or real property for sale and may not further regulate the use of temporary open house or for sale signs that are industry standard size and that are owned or used by the seller or the seller's agent.

2. Open house hours. The association may not limit the hours for an open house for real estate that is for sale in the planned community, except that the association may prohibit an open house being held before 8:00 a.m. or after 6:00 p.m. and may prohibit open house signs on the common areas of the planned community.

3. An owner's or an owner's agent's for rent or for lease sign unless an association's documents prohibit or restrict leasing of a member's property. An association shall not further regulate a for rent or for lease sign or require the use of a particular for rent or for lease sign other than the for rent or for lease sign shall not be any larger than the industry standard size sign of eighteen by twenty-four inches on or in the member's property. If rental or leasing of a member's property is not prohibited or restricted, the association may prohibit an open house for rental or leasing being held before 8:00 a.m. or after 6:00 p.m.

G. Notwithstanding any provision in the community documents, an association shall not prohibit door to door political activity, including solicitations of support or opposition regarding candidates or ballot issues, and shall not prohibit the circulation of political petitions, including candidate nomination petitions or petitions in support of or opposition to an initiative, referendum or recall or other political issue on property normally open to visitors within the association, except that an association may do the following:

1. Restrict or prohibit the door-to-door political activity from sunset to sunrise.

2. Require the prominent display of an identification tag for each person engaged in the activity, along with the prominent identification of the candidate or ballot issue that is the subject of the support or opposition.

H. A planned community shall not make any regulations regarding the number of candidates supported, the number of public officers supported or opposed in a recall or the number of propositions supported or opposed on a political sign.

I. A planned community shall not require political signs to be commercially produced or professionally manufactured or prohibit the utilization of both sides of a political sign.

J. A planned community is not required to comply with subsection G if the planned community restricts vehicular or pedestrian access to the planned community. Nothing in this section requires a planned community to make its common elements other than roadways and sidewalks that are normally open to visitors available for the circulation of political petitions to anyone who is not an owner or resident of the community.

K. An association or managing agent that violates subsection F of this section forfeits and extinguishes the lien rights authorized under section 33-1807 against that member's property for a period of six consecutive months from the date of the violation

33-1809. Parking; public service and public safety emergency vehicles; definition

A. Notwithstanding any provision in the community documents, an association shall not prohibit a resident from parking a motor vehicle on a street or driveway in the planned community if the vehicle is required to be available at designated periods at the person's residence as a condition of the person's employment and either of the following applies:

1. The resident is employed by a public service corporation that is regulated by the corporation commission, an entity regulated by the federal energy regulatory commission or a municipal

utility and the public service corporation or municipal utility is required to prepare for emergency deployments of personnel and equipment for repair or maintenance of natural gas, electrical, telecommunications or water infrastructure, the vehicle has a gross vehicle weight rating of twenty thousand pounds or less and is owned or operated by the public service corporation or municipal utility and the vehicle bears an official emblem or other visible designation of the public service corporation or municipal utility.

2. The resident is employed by a public safety agency, including police or fire service for a federal, state, local or tribal agency or a private fire service provider or an ambulance service provider that is regulated pursuant to title 36, chapter 21.1, and the vehicle has a gross vehicle weight rating of ten thousand pounds or less and bears an official emblem or other visible designation of that agency.

B. For the purposes of this section, "telecommunications" means the transmission of information of the user's choosing between or among points specified by the user without change in the form or content of the information as sent and received. Telecommunications does not include commercial mobile radio services.

33-1810. Board of directors; annual audit

Unless any provision in the planned community documents requires an annual audit by a certified public accountant, the board of directors shall provide for an annual financial audit, review or compilation of the association. The audit, review or compilation shall be completed no later than one hundred eighty days after the end of the association's fiscal year and shall be made available upon request to the members within thirty days after its completion.

33-1811. Board of directors; contracts; conflict

If any contract, decision or other action for compensation taken by or on behalf of the board of directors would benefit any member of the board of directors or any person who is a parent, grandparent, spouse, child or sibling of a member of the board of directors or a parent or spouse of any of those persons, that member of the board of directors shall declare a conflict of interest for that issue. The member shall declare the conflict in an open meeting of the board before the board discusses or takes action on that issue and that member may then vote on that issue. Any contract entered into in violation of this section is void and unenforceable.

33-1812. Proxies; absentee ballots; definition

A. Notwithstanding any provision in the community documents, after termination of the period of declarant control, votes allocated to a unit may not be cast pursuant to a proxy. The association shall provide for votes to be cast in person and by absentee ballot and, in addition, the association may provide for voting by some other form of delivery, including the use of electronic mail and facsimile delivery. Notwithstanding section 10-3708 or the provisions of the community documents, any action taken at an annual, regular or special meeting of the members shall comply with all of the following if absentee ballots or ballots provided by some other form of delivery are used:

1. The ballot shall set forth each proposed action.

2. The ballot shall provide an opportunity to vote for or against each proposed action.

3. The ballot is valid for only one specified election or meeting of the members and expires automatically after the completion of the election or meeting.

4. The ballot specifies the time and date by which the ballot must be delivered to the board of directors in order to be counted, which shall be at least seven days after the date that the board delivers the un-voted ballot to the member.

5. The ballot does not authorize another person to cast votes on behalf of the member.

B. Votes cast by absentee ballot or other form of delivery, including the use of electronic mail and facsimile delivery, are valid for the purpose of establishing a quorum.

C. Notwithstanding subsection A of this section, an association for a timeshare plan as defined in section 32-2197 may permit votes by a proxy that is duly executed by a unit owner.

D. For the purposes of this section, "period of declarant control" means the time during which the declarant or persons designated by the declarant may elect or appoint the members of the board of directors pursuant to the community documents or by virtue of superior voting power.

33-1813. Removal of board member; special meeting

A. Notwithstanding any provision of the declaration or bylaws to the contrary, all of the following apply to a meeting at which a member of the board of directors, other than a member appointed by the declarant, is proposed to be removed from the board of directors:

1. The members of the association who are eligible to vote at the time of the meeting may remove any member of the board of directors, other than a member appointed by the declarant, by a majority vote of those voting on the matter at a meeting of the members.

2. The meeting of the members shall be called pursuant to this section and action may be taken only if a quorum is present.

3. The members of the association may remove any member of the board of directors with or without cause, other than a member appointed by the declarant.

4. For purposes of calling for removal of a member of the board of directors, other than a member appointed by the declarant, the following apply:

   a) In an association with one thousand or fewer members, on receipt of a petition that calls for removal of a member of the board of directors and that is signed by the number of persons who are eligible to vote in the association at the time the person signs the petition equal to at least twenty-five percent of the votes in the association or by the number of persons who are eligible to vote in the association at the time the person signs the petition equal to at least one hundred votes in the association, whichever is less, the board shall call and provide written notice of a special meeting of the association as prescribed by section 33-1804, subsection B.

   b) Notwithstanding section 33-1804, subsection B, in an association with more than one thousand members, on

129

receipt of a petition that calls for removal of a member of the board of directors and that is signed by the number of persons who are eligible to vote in the association at the time the person signs the petition equal to at least ten percent of the votes in the association or by the number of persons who are eligible to vote in the association at the time the person signs the petition equal to at least one thousand votes in the association, whichever is less, the board shall call and provide written notice of a special meeting of the association. The board shall provide written notice of a special meeting as prescribed by section 33-1804, subsection B.

c) The special meeting shall be called, noticed and held within thirty days after receipt of the petition.

d) For purposes of a special meeting called pursuant to this subsection, a quorum is present if the number of owners who are eligible to vote in the association at the time the person attends the meeting equal to at least twenty percent of the votes of the association or the number of persons who are eligible to vote in the association at the time the person attends the meeting equal to at least one thousand votes, whichever is less, is present at the meeting in person or as otherwise permitted by law.

e) If a civil action is filed regarding the removal of a board member, the prevailing party in the civil action shall be awarded its reasonable attorney fees and costs.

f) The board of directors shall retain all documents and other records relating to the proposed removal of the member of the board of directors and any election or other action taken for that director's replacement for at least one year after the date of the special meeting and shall permit members to inspect those documents and records pursuant to section 33-1805.

g) A petition that calls for the removal of the same member of the board of directors shall not be submitted more than once during each term of office for that member.

5. On removal of at least one but fewer than a majority of the members of the board of directors at a special meeting of the membership called pursuant to this subsection, the vacancies shall be filled as provided in the community documents.

6. On removal of a majority of the members of the board of directors at a special meeting of the membership called pursuant to this subsection, or if the community documents do not provide a method for filling board vacancies, the association shall hold an election for the replacement of the removed directors at a separate meeting of the members of the association that is held not later than thirty days after the meeting at which the members of the board of directors were removed.

7. A member of the board of directors who is removed pursuant to this subsection is not eligible to serve on the board of directors again until after the expiration of the removed board member's term of office, unless the community documents specifically provide for a longer period of ineligibility.

8. For an association in which board members are elected from separately designated voting 33-

33-1814. Slum property; professional management

For any residential rental units that have been declared a slum property by the city or town pursuant to section 33-1905 and that are in the planned community, the association is responsible for enforcing any requirement for a licensed property management firm that is imposed by a city or town pursuant to section 33-1906.

33-1815. Association authority; commercial signage

Notwithstanding any provision in the community documents, after an association has approved a commercial sign, including its registered trademark that is located on properties zoned for commercial use in the planned community, the association, including any subsequently elected board of directors, may not revoke or modify its approval of that sign if the owner or operator of the sign has received approval for the sign from the local or county governing body with jurisdiction over the sign.

33-1816. Solar energy devices; reasonable restrictions; fees and costs

A. Notwithstanding any provision in the community documents, an association shall not prohibit the installation or use of a solar energy device as defined in section 44-1761.

B. An association may adopt reasonable rules regarding the placement of a solar energy device if those rules do not prevent the installation, impair the functioning of the device or restrict its use or adversely affect the cost or efficiency of the device.

C. Notwithstanding any provision of the community documents, the court shall award reasonable attorney fees and costs to any party who substantially prevails in an action against the board of directors of the association for a violation of this section.

33-1817. Declaration amendment; design, architectural committees;

Review

Notwithstanding any provision in the community documents:

1. Membership on a design review committee, an architectural committee or a committee that performs similar functions, however denominated, for the planned community shall include at least one member of the board of directors who shall serve as chairperson of the committee.

2. For new construction of the main residential structure on a lot or for rebuilds of the main residential structure on a lot and only in a planned community that has enacted design guidelines, architectural guidelines or other similar rules, however denominated, and if the association documents permit the association to charge the member a security deposit and the association requires the member to pay a security deposit to secure completion of the member's construction project or compliance with approved plans, all of the following apply:

a) The deposit shall be placed in a trust account with the following instructions:

i) The cost of the trust account shall be shared equally between the association and the member.

ii) If the construction project is abandoned, the board of directors may determine the appropriate use of any deposit monies.

iii) Any interest earned on the refundable security deposit shall become part of the security deposit.

b) The association or the design review committee must hold a final design approval meeting for the purpose of issuing approval of the plans, and the member or member's agent must have the opportunity to attend the meeting. If the plans are approved, the association's design review representative shall provide written acknowledgement that the approved plans, including any approved amendments, are in compliance with all rules and guidelines in effect at the time of the approval and that the refund of the deposit requires that construction be completed in accordance with those approved plans.

c) The association must provide for at least two on-site formal reviews during construction for the purpose of determining compliance with the approved plans. The member or member's agent shall be provided the opportunity to attend both formal reviews. Within five business days after the formal reviews, the association shall cause a written report to be provided to the member or member's agent specifying any deficiencies, violations or unapproved variations from the approved plans as amended that have come to the attention of the association.

d) Within thirty business days after the second formal review, the association shall provide to the member a copy of the written report specifying any deficiencies, violations or unapproved variations from the approved plans as amended that have come to the attention of the association. If the written report does not specify any deficiencies, violations or unapproved variations from the approved plans, as amended, that have come to the attention of the association, the association shall promptly release the deposit monies to the member. If the report identifies any deficiencies, violations or unapproved variations from the approved plans, as amended, the association may hold the deposit for one hundred eighty days or until receipt of a subsequent report of construction compliance, whichever is less. If a report of construction compliance is received before the one hundred eightieth day, the association shall promptly release the deposit monies to the member. If a compliance report is not received within one hundred eighty days, the association shall release the deposit monies promptly from the trust account to the association.

e) Neither the approval of the plans nor the approval of the actual construction by the association or the design review committee shall constitute a representation or warranty that the plans or construction comply with applicable governmental requirements or applicable engineering, design or safety standards. The association in its discretion may release all or any part of the deposit to the member before receiving a compliance report. Release of the deposit to the member does not constitute a representation or warranty from the association that the construction complies with the approved plans.

33-1818. Community authority over public roadways; applicability

A. Notwithstanding any provision in the community documents, after the period of declarant control, an association has no authority over and shall not regulate any roadway for which the ownership has been dedicated to or is otherwise held by a governmental entity.

B. This section applies only to those planned communities for which the declaration is recorded after December 31, 2014.

SECTION VIII.
NON-PROFIT CORPORATION ACT

ARS 10-3101

When people make donations to non-profits, they want to know that their money goes to good use.

~ Sam Simon (1955-2015)
American Director

CHAPTER 24
GENERAL PROVISIONS

ARTICLE 1 SHORT TITLE

§ **10-3101** Short title

§ **10-3102** Reservation of power to amend or repeal

ARTICLE 3 ARIZONA CORPORATION COMMISSION

§ **10-3130** Power

ARTICLE 4 DEFINITIONS, NOTICE, PRIVATE FOUNDATION JUDICIAL RELIEF AND RELIGIOUS ORGANIZATIONS

CHAPTER 25
INCORPORATION

ARTICLE 1 INCORPORATION

CHAPTER 26
PURPOSES AND POWERS

ARTICLE 1 GENERAL PROVISIONS

CHAPTER 28
OFFICE AND AGENT

ARTICLE 1
PLACE OF BUSINESS AND AGENT

CHAPTER 29
MEMBERS AND MEMBERSHIPS

ARTICLE 1
ADMISSION OF MEMBERS

§ **10-3601** Admission

§ **10-3602** Consideration

§ **10-3603** No requirement of members

ARTICLE 2 TYPES OF MEMBERSHIPS-MEMBERS'
RIGHTS AND OBLIGATIONS

§ **10-3610** Difference in rights and obligations of members

§ **10-3611** Transfers

§ **10-3612** Member's liability to third parties

§ **10-3613** Member's liability for dues, assessments and fees

§ **10-3614** Creditor's action against member

ARTICLE 3
RESIGNATION AND TERMINATION

§ **10-3620** Resignation

§ **10-3621** Termination, expulsion and suspension

§ **10-3622** Purchase of memberships

CHAPTER 30
MEMBERS' MEETINGS AND VOTING

ARTICLE 1
MEETINGS AND ACTION WITHOUT MEETINGS

ARTICLE 2
VOTING

CHAPTER 31
DIRECTORS AND OFFICERS
NON-PROFIT CORPORATIONS

ARTICLE 1
BOARD OF DIRECTORS

ARTICLE 2
MEETINGS AND ACTION OF THE BOARD

ARTICLE 3
STANDARDS OF CONDUCT

ARTICLE 4
OFFICERS

ARTICLE 5
INDEMNIFICATION

ARTICLE 6
DIRECTOR'S CONFLICTING INTEREST TRANSACTIONS

CHAPTER 33
AMENDMENT OF ARTICLES OF INCORPORATION AND BYLAWS

ARTICLE 1
ARTICLES OF INCORPORATION

ARTICLE 2
BYLAWS

ARTICLE 3
ARTICLES OF INCORPORATION AND BYLAWS

§ **10-11030** Approval by third persons

§ **10-11031** Amendment terminating members or redeeming or canceling membership

CHAPTER 36
DISTRIBUTIONS

§ **10-11301** Prohibited distributions

§ **10-11302** Authorized distributions

CHAPTER 39
RECORDS AND REPORTS

ARTICLE 1 RECORDS

§ **10-11601** Corporate records

§ **10-11602** Inspection of records by members; applicability

§ **10-11603** Scope of inspection rights; charge

§ **10-11604** Court ordered inspection

§ **10-11605** Limitations on use of membership list; applicability

§ **10-11620** Financial statements for members

§ **10-11621** Report of indemnification to members

§ **10-11622** Annual report

CHAPTER 40
TRANSITION PROVISIONS

Chapters 24 through 40 shall be known—and may be cited as— the Arizona Nonprofit Corporation Act.

ARTICLE 1
GENERAL PROVISIONS

§ 10-11701 Application to existing domestic

10-3101.Short title

10-3102. Reservation of power to amend or repeal

The legislature has the power to amend or repeal all or part of this act at any time and all domestic and foreign corporations subject to this act are governed by the amendment or repeal.

10-3130. Powers

The commission has the power and authority reasonably necessary to enable it to administer this title efficiently and to perform the duties imposed on it by this title, including the power and authority to make rules and regulations for those purposes.

10-3140. Definitions

In chapters 24 through 40 of this title, unless the context otherwise requires:

1. "Acknowledged" or "acknowledgment" means either an acknowledgment pursuant to title 33, chapter 4, article 5 or the signature, without more, of the person or persons signing the instrument, in which case the signature or signatures constitute the affirmation or acknowledgment of the

signatory, under penalties of perjury, that the instrument is the act and deed of the signatory and that the facts stated in the instrument are true.

2. "Act of the board of directors" means either:

c) An act of the majority of the directors present at a

i. duly called meeting at which a quorum is present, unless the act of a greater number is required by chapters 24 through 40 of this title, the articles of incorporation or the bylaws.

ii. Action taken by written consent of the directors in accordance with chapters 24 through 40 of this title.

3. "Act of the members" means either:

a) An act adopted or rejected by a majority of the votes represented and voting at a duly held meeting at which a quorum is present where affirmative votes also constitute a majority of the required quorum unless a greater number of votes is required by chapters 24 through 40 of this title, the articles of incorporation or the bylaws.

b) An action taken by written consent of the members in accordance with chapters 24 through 40 of this title.

c) An action taken written ballot of the members in accordance with this chapter.

4. "Address" means a mailing address.

5. "Affiliate" means a person that directly or indirectly through one or more intermediaries controls, is controlled by or is under common control with the person specified.

6. "Articles of incorporation" means the original or restated articles of incorporation or articles of merger and all amendments to the articles of incorporation or merger and includes amended and restated articles of incorporation and articles of amendment and merger.

7. "Board," " board of directors," or " board of trustees" means the group of persons vested with the direction of the affairs of the corporation irrespective of the name by which the group is designated, except that no person or group of persons shall be deemed to be the board of directors solely

because of powers delegated to that person or group pursuant to section 10-3801, subsection C.

8. "Business day" means a day that is not a Saturday, a Sunday or any other legal holiday in this state.

9. "Bylaws" means the code of rules adopted for the regulation or management of the affairs of the corporation irrespective of the name by which those rules are designated.

10. "Certificate of disclosure" means the certificate of disclosure described in section 10-3202.

11. "Class" refers to a group of memberships that have the same rights with respect to voting, dissolution, redemption and transfer. Rights are the same if they are determined by a formula applied uniformly.

12. "Commission" means the Arizona corporation commission.

13. "Conspicuous" means so written that a reasonable person against whom the writing is to operate should have noticed it. For example, printing in italics, boldface or contrasting color or typing in capitals or underlined is conspicuous.

14. "Corporation" or " domestic corporation" means a nonprofit corporation that is not a foreign corporation and that is incorporated under or subject to chapters 24 through 40 of this title.

15. "Corporation sole" means a corporation formed pursuant and subject to chapter 42, article 1 of this title.

16. "Court" means the superior court of this state.

17. "Delegates" means those persons elected or appointed to vote in a representative assembly for the election of a director or directors or on other matters.

18. "Deliver" includes mail, private courier, fax or electronic mail.

19. "Delivery" means actual receipt by the person or entity to which directed.

20 "Directors" or " trustees" means individuals, designated in the articles of incorporation or bylaws or elected by the incorporators, and their successors and individuals elected or

appointed by any other name or title to act as members of the board.

21. "Dissolved" means the status of a corporation on either:

    a) Effectiveness of articles of dissolution pursuant to section 10-11403, subsection B or section 10-11421, subsection B.

    b) A decree pursuant to section 10-11433, subsection B becoming final.

22. "Distribution" means a direct or indirect transfer of money or other property or incurrence of indebtedness by a corporation to or for the benefit of its members in respect of any of its membership interests. A distribution may be in the form of any of the following:

    a) A declaration of payment of a dividend.

    b) Any purchase, redemption or other acquisition of membership interests.

    c) A distribution of indebtedness.

    d) Otherwise.

23. "Effective date of notice" is prescribed in section 10-3141.

24. "Electronic mail" means an electronic record as defined in section 44-7002 and that is sent pursuant to section 44-7015, subsection A.

25. "Employee" means an officer, director or other person who is employed by the corporation.

26. "Entity" includes a corporation, foreign corporation, not for profit corporation, business corporation, foreign business corporation, profit and not for profit unincorporated association, close corporation, corporation sole, limited liability company or registered limited liability partnership, a professional corporation, association or limited liability company or registered limited liability partnership, a business trust, estate, partnership, trust or joint venture, two or more persons having a joint or common economic interest, any person other than an individual and a state, the United States and a foreign government.

27. "Executed by the corporation" means executed by manual or facsimile signature on behalf of the corporation by a duly authorized officer or, if the corporation is in the hands of a receiver or trustee, by the receiver or trustee.

28. "Filing" means the commission completing the following procedure with respect to any document delivered for that purpose:

   a) Determining that the filing fee requirements of this title have been satisfied.

   b) Determining that the document appears in all respects to conform to the requirements of chapters 24 through 40 of this title.

   c) On making the determinations, endorsement of the word " filed" with the applicable date on or attached to the document and the return of copies to the person who delivered the document or the person's representative.

29. "Foreign Corporation" means a corporation that is organized under a law other than the law of this state and that would be a nonprofit corporation if formed under the laws of this state.

30. "Governmental subdivision" includes an authority, county, district, municipality and political subdivision.

31. " Includes" and " including" denotes a partial definition.

32. "Individual" includes the estate of an incompetent individual.

33. "Insolvent" means inability of a corporation to pay its debts as they become due in the usual course of its business.

34. "Known place of business" means the known place of business required to be maintained pursuant to section 10-3501.

35. "Mail", "to mail" or" have mailed" means to deposit or have deposited a communication in the United States mail with first class postage prepaid.

36. "Means" denotes an exhaustive definition.

37. "Member" means, without regard to what a person is called in the articles of incorporation or bylaws, any person or persons who, pursuant to a provision of a corporation's

articles of incorporation or bylaws, have the right to vote for the election of a director or directors. A person is not a member by virtue of any of the following:

a) Any rights that person has as a delegate.

b) Any rights that person has to designate a director or directors.

c) Any rights that person has as a director.

d) Being referred to as a member in the articles of incorporation, bylaws or any other document, if the person does not have the right to vote for the election of a director or directors.

39. "Membership" refers to the rights and obligations a member or members have pursuant to a corporation's articles of incorporation, bylaws and chapters 24 through 40 of this title.

40. "Newspaper" has the same meaning prescribed in section 39-201.

41. "Notice" and "notify" are prescribed in section 10-3141.

42. "Person" includes individual and entity.

43. "President" means that officer designated as the president in the articles of incorporation or bylaws or, if not so designated, that officer authorized in the articles of incorporation, bylaws or otherwise to perform the functions of the chief executive officer, irrespective of the name by which designated.

44. "Principal office" means the office, in or out of this state, so designated in the annual report where the principal executive offices of a domestic or foreign corporation are located or in any other document executed by the corporation by an officer and delivered to the commission for filing. If an office has not been so designated, principal office means the known place of business of the corporation.

45. "Proceeding" includes a civil suit and a criminal, administrative and investigatory action.

46. "Publish" means to publish in a newspaper of general circulation in the county of the known place of business for three consecutive publications.

47. "Record date" means the date, if any, established under chapter 29 or 30 of this title on which a corporation determines the identity of its members and their membership interests for purposes of chapters 24 through 40 of this title. The determinations shall be made as of the close of business on the record date unless another time for doing so is specified when the record date is fixed.

48. "Secretary" means that officer designated as the secretary in the articles of incorporation or bylaws or that officer authorized in the articles of incorporation, the bylaws or otherwise to perform the functions of secretary, irrespective of the name by which designated.

49. "State" if referring to a part of the United States, includes a state and commonwealth and their agencies and governmental subdivisions and a territory and insular possession of the United States and their agencies and governmental subdivisions.

50. "Treasurer" means that officer designated as the treasurer in the articles of incorporation or bylaws or that officer authorized in the articles of incorporation, bylaws or otherwise to perform the functions of treasurer, irrespective of the name by which designated.

51. "United States" includes a district, authority, bureau, commission and department and any other agency of the United States.

52. "Vice-president" means an officer designated as a vice-president in the articles of incorporation or bylaws or an officer authorized in the articles of incorporation, the bylaws or otherwise to perform the functions of a vice-president, irrespective of the name by which designated.

53. "Vote" includes authorization by written ballot and written consent.

54. "Voting power" means the total number of votes entitled to be cast for the election of directors at the time the determination of voting power is made, excluding a vote that is contingent on the happening of a condition or event that has not occurred at the time. If a class is entitled to vote as a class for directors, the determination of voting power of the class shall be based on the percentage of the number of

directors the class is entitled to elect out of the total number of authorized directors.

10-3141. Notice

A. Notice under chapters 24 through 40 of this title must be in writing unless oral notice is reasonable under the circumstances. Oral notice is not permitted if written notice is required under chapters 24 through 40 of this title.

B. Notice may be communicated in person, by telephone, telegraph, teletype, fax, electronic mail or other form of wire or wireless communication, or by mail or private carrier. If these forms of personal notice are impracticable, notice may be communicated by a newspaper of general circulation in the area where published or by radio, television or other form of public broadcast communication.

C. Written notice by a domestic or foreign corporation to its members or directors, if in comprehensible form, is effective when mailed, if correctly addressed to the member's address shown on the corporation's current list of members or directors. Notice given by electronic mail, if in comprehensible form, is effective when directed to an electronic mail address shown on the corporation's current list of members or directors.

D. A written notice or report by a domestic or foreign corporation to its members delivered as part of a newsletter, magazine or other publication regularly sent to members shall constitute a written notice or report if addressed or delivered to the member's address shown in the corporation's current list of members, or in the case of members who are residents of the same household and who have the same address in the corporation's current list of members, if addressed or delivered to one of such members, at the address appearing on the current list of members.

E. Written notice to a domestic or foreign corporation that is authorized to transact business in this state, other than in its capacity as a member, may be addressed to its statutory agent at its known place of business or to the corporation or its secretary at its principal office shown in its most recent annual report on file with the commission, or in the case of a foreign corporation that has not yet delivered an annual report in its application for a certificate of authority.

F. Except as provided in subsection C, written notice, if in a comprehensible form, is effective at the earliest of the following:

1. When received.

   2. Five days after its deposit in the United States mail as evidenced by the postmark, if mailed postpaid and correctly addressed.

   3. On the date shown on the return receipt, if sent by registered or certified mail, return receipt requested, and if the receipt is signed by or on behalf of the addressee.

G. Oral notice is effective when communicated if communicated in a comprehensible manner.

H. If chapters 24 through 40 of this title prescribe notice requirements for particular circumstances, those requirements govern. If articles of incorporation or bylaws prescribe notice requirements that are not inconsistent with this section or other provisions of chapters 24 through 40 of this title those requirements govern.

10-3160. Judicial relief

A. If for any reason it is impractical or impossible for any corporation to call or conduct a meeting of its members, delegates or directors, or otherwise obtain their consent, in the manner prescribed by its articles of incorporation, bylaws, or chapters 24 through 40 of this title, on petition of a director, officer, delegate or member, the court may order that such a meeting be called or that a written ballot or other form of obtaining the vote of members, delegates or directors be authorized, in such a manner as the court finds fair and equitable under the circumstances.

B. The court, in an order issued pursuant to this section, shall provide for a method of notice reasonably designed to give actual notice to all persons who would be entitled to notice of a meeting held pursuant to the articles of incorporation, bylaws and chapters 24 through 40 of this title, whether or not the method results in actual notice to all such persons or conforms to the notice requirements that would otherwise apply. In a proceeding under this section the court may determine who the members or directors are.

C. The order issued pursuant to this section may dispense with any requirement relating to the holding of or voting at meetings or obtaining votes, including any requirement as to quorums or as to the number or percentage of votes needed for approval, than would otherwise be imposed by the articles of incorporation, bylaws, or chapters 24 through 40 of this title.

D. If practical, any order issued pursuant to this section shall limit the subject matter of meetings or other forms of consent authorized to items, including amendments to the articles of incorporation or bylaws, the resolution of which will or may enable the corporation to

E. Notwithstanding subsection D, an order under this section may also authorize the obtaining of the votes and approvals that are necessary for the dissolution, merger or sale of assets.

F. Any meeting or other method of obtaining the vote of members, delegates or directors conducted pursuant to an order issued under this section, and that complies with all the provisions of that order, is a valid meeting or vote and shall have the same force and effect as if it complied with every requirement imposed by the articles of incorporation, bylaws and chapters 24 through 40 of this title.

10-3201. Incorporators

One or more persons may act as the incorporator or incorporators of a corporation by delivering articles of incorporation and a certificate of disclosure to the commission for filing.

10-3202. Articles of incorporation

A. The articles of incorporation shall set forth:

1. A corporate name for the corporation that satisfies the requirements of section 10-3401.

2. A brief statement of the character of affairs that the corporation initially intends to conduct. This statement does not limit the affairs that the corporation may conduct.

3. The name and address of each person who is to serve as a director until a successor is elected and qualifies.

4. The name, street address and signature of the corporation's statutory agent.

5. The street address of the known place of business for the corporation, if different from that of its statutory agent.

6. The name and address of each incorporator.

7. Whether or not the corporation will have members.

8. Any provision elected by the incorporators that under chapters 24 through 40 of this title or any other law of this state may be elected only by specific inclusion in the articles of incorporation.

9. The signatures of all incorporators.

B. The articles of incorporation may set forth:

1. A provision eliminating or limiting the liability of a director to the corporation or its members for money damages for any action taken or any failure to take any action as a director, except liability for any of the following:

a) The amount of a financial benefit received by a director to which the director is not entitled.

b) An intentional infliction of harm on the corporation or the members.

c) A violation of section 10-3833.

d) An intentional violation of criminal law.

2. A provision permitting or making obligatory indemnification of a director for liability, as defined in section 10-3850, to any person for any action taken, or any failure to take any action, as a director, except liability for any of the exceptions described in paragraph 1 of this subsection.

3. Any other provision, not inconsistent with law.

C. The articles of incorporation need not set forth any of the corporate powers enumerated in chapters 24 through 40 of this title.

D. The certificate of disclosure shall set forth all of the following:

1. The following information regarding all persons who at the time of its delivery are officers, directors, trustees and incorporators:

a) Whether any of the persons have been convicted of a felony involving a transaction in securities, consumer fraud or antitrust in any state or federal jurisdiction within the seven year period immediately preceding the execution of the certificate.

b) Whether any of the persons have been convicted of a felony, the essential elements of which consisted of fraud, misrepresentation, theft by false pretenses or restraint of trade or monopoly in any state or federal jurisdiction within the seven year period immediately preceding the execution of the certificate.

c) Whether any of the persons are or have been subject to an injunction, judgment, decree or permanent order of any state or federal court entered within the seven year period immediately preceding the execution of the certificate, if the injunction, judgment, decree or permanent order involved any of the following:

   i. The violation of fraud or registration provisions of the securities laws of that jurisdiction.

   ii. The violation of consumer fraud laws of that jurisdiction.

   iii. The violation of the antitrust or restraint of trade laws of that jurisdiction.

d) With regard to any of the persons who have been convicted of the crimes or who are the subject of the judicial action described in subdivisions (a), (b) and (c) of this paragraph, information regarding:

   i. Identification of the persons, including present full name, all prior names or aliases, including full birth name, present home address, all prior addresses for the

   ii. immediately preceding seven year period and date and location of birth.

   iii. The nature and description of each conviction or judicial action, the date and location, the court and public agency involved, and the file or case number of the case.

2. A brief statement disclosing whether any persons who at the time of its delivery are officers, directors, trustees and

incorporators and who have served in any such capacity in any other corporation on the bankruptcy or receivership of the other corporation. If so, for each corporation, the certificate shall include:

a) The names and addresses of each corporation and the person or persons involved.

b) The state in which each corporation:

   i. Was incorporated.

   ii. Transacted business.

c) The dates of corporate operation.

3. The signatures of all the incorporators.

4. The date of its execution, which shall be not more than thirty days before its delivery to the commission.

5. A declaration by each signer that the signer swears to its contents under penalty of law.

E. The certificate of disclosure may set forth the name and address of any other person whom the incorporator or incorporators choose to be the subject of those disclosures required under subsection D, paragraph 1 of this section.

F. If within sixty days after delivering the articles of incorporation and certificate of disclosure to the commission any person becomes an officer, director or trustee and the person was not the subject of the disclosures set forth in the certificate of disclosure, the incorporator or incorporators or, if the organization of the corporation has been completed as provided in section 10-3205, the corporation shall execute and deliver to the commission within the sixty day period a declaration, sworn to under penalty of law, setting forth all information required by subsection D, paragraph 1 of this section, regarding the person. If the incorporator or incorporators or, as applicable, the corporation fails to comply with this subsection, the commission may administratively dissolve the corporation pursuant to section 10-11421.

G. If any of the persons described in subsection D, paragraph 1 of this section have been convicted of the crimes or are the subject of the judicial action described in subsection D, paragraph 1 of this section, the commission may direct detailed interrogatories to the persons requiring any additional relevant information deemed necessary by the commission. The interrogatories shall be completely answered within thirty days after mailing of the interrogatories. With respect to corporations incorporating or seeking authority to conduct affairs, articles of incorporation or an application for authority shall not be filed until all outstanding interrogatories have been answered to the satisfaction of the commission. With respect to existing domestic and foreign corporations, if the interrogatories are not answered as provided in this subsection or the answers to the interrogatories otherwise indicate proper grounds for an administrative dissolution, the commission shall initiate an administrative dissolution in accordance with chapters 24 through 40 of this title.

H. On a quarterly updated basis, the commission shall provide to the attorney general a list of all persons who are convicted of the crimes or who are the subject of the judicial action described in subsection D, paragraph 1 of this section as indicated by the certificate of disclosure filed during the preceding three months.

I. Any person who executed or contributed information for a certificate of disclosure and who intentionally makes any untrue statement of material fact or withholds any material fact with regard to the information required in subsection D, paragraph 1 of this section is guilty of a class 6 felony.

10-3203. Incorporation

A. Unless a delayed effective date is specified in the articles of incorporation, incorporation occurs and the corporate existence begins when the articles of incorporation and certificate of disclosure are delivered to the commission for filing.

B. The commission's filing of the articles of incorporation and certificate of disclosure is conclusive proof that the incorporators satisfied all conditions precedent to incorporation except in a proceeding by the state to cancel or revoke the incorporation or involuntarily dissolve the corporation pursuant to chapter 37 of this title.

C. Subject to section 10-3124, if the commission determines that the requirements of chapters 24 through 42 of this title for filing have not been met, the articles of incorporation and certificate of disclosure shall not be filed and the corporate existence terminates at the time the commission completes the determination. If the corporate existence is terminated pursuant to this subsection, sections 10-11404, 10-11405 and 10-11406 apply.

D. Within sixty days after the commission approves the filing, a copy of the articles of incorporation shall be published. An affidavit evidencing the publication may be filed with the commission.

10-3204. Liability for non-corporate transactions

All persons purporting to act as or on behalf of a corporation with actual knowledge that no corporation exists under chapters 24 through 40 of this title are jointly and severally liable to the extent not precluded by section 12-2506 for all liabilities created while so acting.

10-3205. Organization of corporation

After incorporation the board of directors shall hold an organizational meeting at the call of a majority of the directors to complete the organization of the corporation by appointing officers, adopting bylaws, and carrying on any other business brought before the meeting.

10-3206. Bylaws

A. The board of directors of a corporation shall adopt initial bylaws for the corporation.

B. The bylaws of a corporation may contain any provision for regulating and managing the affairs of the corporation that is not inconsistent with law or the articles of incorporation.

10-3207. Emergency bylaws

A. Unless the articles of incorporation provide otherwise, the board of directors of a corporation may adopt bylaws to be effective only in an emergency defined in subsection D of this section. The emergency bylaws are subject to amendment or repeal by the members and may make all provisions necessary for managing the corporation during the emergency, including all of the following:

1. Procedures for calling a meeting of the board of directors.

2. Quorum requirements for the meeting.

3. Designation of additional or substitute directors.

B. All provisions of the regular bylaws consistent with the emergency bylaws remain effective during the emergency. The emergency bylaws are not effective after the emergency ends.

C. Corporate action taken in good faith in accordance with the emergency bylaws both:

1. Binds the corporation.

2. May not be used to impose liability on a corporate director, officer, employee or agent.

D. An emergency exists for purposes of this section if a quorum of the corporation's directors cannot readily be assembled because of a local emergency, a state of emergency or a state of war emergency, all as defined in section 26-301.

10-3301. Purposes

Subject to any limitations or requirements contained in its articles of incorporation or in any other applicable law, a corporation shall have the purpose of engaging in and may engage in any lawful activity including the practice of medicine as defined in section 32-1401 or the practice of dentistry as described in section 32-1202, or both, provided that the corporation engages in the practice of medicine or dentistry only through individuals licensed to practice in this state. This section does not alter any law or change any liability that might otherwise be applicable to the relationship between persons furnishing a professional service and persons receiving a professional service, including liability arising from that relationship.

10-3302. General powers

Unless its articles of incorporation provide otherwise, every corporation has perpetual duration and succession in its corporate name and has the same powers as an individual to do all things necessary or convenient to carry out its affairs including power to:

1. Sue and be sued, complain and defend in its corporate name.

2. Have a corporate seal, which may be altered at will, and to use it, or a facsimile of it, by impressing or affixing or in any other manner reproducing it.

3. Make and amend bylaws, not inconsistent with its articles of incorporation or with the laws of this state, for regulating and managing the affairs of the corporation.

4. Purchase, receive, lease or otherwise acquire and own, hold, improve, use and otherwise deal with real or personal property or any interest in property wherever located.

5. Sell, convey, mortgage, pledge, lease, exchange and otherwise dispose of all or any part of its property.

6. Purchase, receive, subscribe for or otherwise acquire, own, hold, vote, use, sell, mortgage, lend, pledge or otherwise dispose of and deal with shares or other interests in or obligations of any entity.

7. Make contracts and guarantees, incur liabilities, borrow monies, issue its notes, bonds and other obligations, which may be convertible into or include the option to purchase other securities of the corporation, and secure any of its obligations by mortgage, deed of trust, security agreement, pledge or other encumbrance of any of its property, franchises or income.

8. Issue any bond, debenture or debt security of the corporation by causing one or more officers designated in the bylaws or by the board of directors to sign the bond, debenture or debt security either manually or in facsimile and, if deemed necessary or appropriate by the officers, by causing its authentication, countersignature or registration, either manually or in facsimile, by a trustee, transfer agent or registrar other than the corporation itself or an employee of the corporation. If an officer who has signed, either manually or in facsimile, a bond, debenture or debt security as provided in this paragraph ceases for any reason to be an officer before the security is issued, the corporation may issue the security with the same effect as if the officer were still in office at the date of issue.

9. Lend monies, invest and reinvest its monies and receive and hold real and personal property as security for repayment, except as limited by section 10-3833.

10. Be a promoter, incorporator, partner, member, associate or manager of any entity.

11. Conduct its activities, locate offices and exercise the powers granted by chapters 24 through 40 of this title within or without this state.

12. Elect or appoint directors, officers, employees and agents of the corporation, define their duties, fix their compensation and lend them monies and credit.

13. Pay pensions and establish pension plans, pension trusts and other benefit or incentive plans for any of its or its affiliates' current or former directors, officers, employees and agents.

14. Eliminate or limit the liability of its directors in the manner and to the extent provided by section 10-3202 and chapter 31, article 5 of this title.

15. Make payments or donations not inconsistent with law for the public welfare or for charitable, religious, scientific or educational purposes and for other purposes that further the corporate interest.

16. Impose dues, assessments, admission and transfer fees on its members.

17. Establish conditions for admission of members, admit members and issue memberships.

18. Carry on a business.

19. Transact any lawful activity that will aid governmental policy.

20. Do any other act not inconsistent with law that furthers the activities and affairs of the corporation?

10-3303. Emergency powers

A. In anticipation of or during an emergency as prescribed in subsection D of this section, the board of directors of a corporation may:

1. Modify lines of succession to accommodate the incapacity of any director, officer, employee or agent.

2. Relocate the principal office, designate alternative principal offices or regional offices or authorize the officers to do so.

B. During an emergency as prescribed in subsection D of this section, unless emergency bylaws provide otherwise:

  1. Notice of a meeting of the board of directors need be given only to those directors whom it is practicable to reach and may be given in any practicable manner, including by publication and radio.

  2. One or more officers of the corporation present at a meeting of the board of directors may be deemed to be directors for the meeting, in order of rank and within the same rank in order of seniority, as necessary to achieve a quorum.

B. Corporate action taken in good faith during an emergency under this section to further the ordinary affairs of the corporation:

  1. Binds the corporation.

  2. May not be used to impose liability on a corporate director, officer, employee or agent.

C. An emergency exists for purposes of this section if a quorum of the corporation's directors cannot readily be assembled because of a local emergency, a state of emergency or a state of war emergency all as defined in section 26-301.

10-3304. Validity of actions

A. Except as provided in subsection B of this section, the validity of corporate action shall not be challenged on the ground that the corporation lacks or lacked power to act.

B. A corporation's power to act may be challenged by any of the following:

  1. In a proceeding by members of a corporation that is not a condominium association as defined in section 33-1202, or a planned community association as defined in section 33-1802, having at least ten per cent or more of the voting power or by at least fifty members, unless a lesser percentage or number is provided in the articles of incorporation, against the corporation to enjoin the act.

163

2. In a proceeding by any member of a condominium or a planned community association against the corporation to enjoin the act pursuant to title 12, chapter 10, article 1.

3. In a proceeding by the corporation, directly, derivatively or through any receiver, trustee or other legal representative, against an incumbent or former director, officer, employee or agent of the corporation.

C. In a member's proceeding under subsection B, paragraph 1 of this section to enjoin an unauthorized corporate act, the court may enjoin or set aside the act, if equitable and if all affected persons are parties to the proceeding, and may award damages for loss, other than anticipated profits, suffered by the corporation or another party because of enjoining the unauthorized act.

10-3501. Known place of business and statutory agent

Each corporation shall continuously maintain in this state both:

1. A known place of business that may be the address of its statutory agent.

2. A statutory agent who may be either:

a) An individual who resides in this state.

b) A domestic business or nonprofit corporation formed under this title.

c) A foreign business or nonprofit corporation authorized to transact business or conduct affairs in this state.

d) A limited liability company formed under title 29.

e) A limited liability company authorized to transact business in this state.

10-3502. Change of known place of business and statutory agent

A. A corporation may change its known place of business or statutory agent by delivering to the commission for filing a statement of change that may be the annual report and that sets forth:

1. The name of the corporation.

2. The street address of its current known place of business.

3. If the current known place of business is to be changed, the street address of the new known place of business.

4. The name and street address of its current statutory agent.

5. If the current statutory agent is to be changed, the name and street address of the new statutory agent and the new agent's written consent to the appointment.

B. The statement of change shall be executed by the corporation by an officer and delivered to the commission. The change or changes set forth in the statement of change are effective on delivery to the commission for filing.

C. If the statutory agent changes its street address, it shall give written notice to the corporation of the change and sign, either manually or in facsimile, and deliver to the commission for filing a statement that complies with the requirements of subsection A and that recites that the corporation has been given written notice of the change. The change or changes set forth in the statement are effective on delivery to the commission for filing.

10-3503. Resignation of statutory agent

A. A statutory agent may resign its agency appointment by signing and delivering to the commission for filing the signed original statement of resignation. The statement may include a statement that the known place of business is also discontinued. The statutory agent shall give written notice of its resignation to the corporation at an address other than the statutory agent's address.

B. After filing the statement, the commission shall mail one copy to the corporation at its known place of business, if not discontinued, and another copy to the corporation at its principal office.

C. The agency appointment is terminated and, if so provided in the statement, the known place of business is discontinued on the thirty-first day after the date on which the statement was delivered to the commission for filing.

10-3504. Service on corporation

A. The statutory agent appointed by a corporation is an agent of the corporation on whom process, notice or demand that is required or permitted by law to be served on the corporation may be

165

served and that, when so served, is lawful personal service on the corporation.

B. If a corporation fails to appoint or maintain a statutory agent at the address shown on the records of the commission, the commission is an agent of the corporation on whom any process, notice or demand may be served. Pursuant to the Arizona rules of civil procedure, service on the commission of any process, notice or demand for an entity that is registered pursuant to this title shall be made by delivering to and leaving with the commission duplicate copies of the process, notice or demand, and the commission shall immediately cause one of the copies of the process, notice or demand to be forwarded by mail, addressed to the corporation at its known place of business. Service made on the commission is returnable pursuant to applicable law relative to personal service on the corporation. If service is made on the commission, whether under this chapter or a rule of court, the corporation has thirty days to respond in addition to the time otherwise provided by law.

C. The commission shall keep a permanent record of all processes, notices and demands served on it under this section and shall record in the record the time of the service and its action with reference to the service.

D. Notice required to be served on a corporation pursuant to section 10-11421 or 10-11422 may be served:

1. By mail addressed to the statutory agent of the corporation or, if the corporation fails to appoint and maintain a statutory agent, addressed to the known place of business required to be maintained pursuant to section 10-3501.

2. Pursuant to the rules for service of process authorized by the Arizona rules of civil procedure.

10-3601. Admission

A. The articles of incorporation or bylaws may establish criteria or procedures for admission of members and continuation of membership.

B. No person shall be admitted as a member without that person's consent. Consent may be express or implied.

10-3602. Consideration

Except as provided in its articles of incorporation or bylaws, a corporation may admit members for no consideration or for such consideration as is determined by the board.

10-3603. No requirement of members

A corporation is not required to have members.

10-3610. Difference in rights and obligations of members

All members have the same rights and obligations with respect to voting, dissolution, redemption and transfer, unless the articles of incorporation or bylaws establish classes of membership with different rights or obligations or otherwise provide. All members have the same rights and obligations with respect to any other matters, except as set forth in or authorized by the articles of incorporation or bylaws.

10-3611. Transfers

A. Except as set forth in or authorized by the articles of incorporation or bylaws, no member of a corporation may transfer a membership or any right arising from that membership.

B. If transfer rights are provided, no restriction on them is binding with respect to a member holding a membership issued prior to the adoption of the restriction unless the restriction is approved by the members and the affected member.

10-3612. Member's liability to third parties

A member of a corporation is not personally liable for the acts, debts, liabilities or obligations of the corporation.

10-3613. Member's liability for dues, assessments and fees

A. A member may become liable to the corporation for dues, assessments and fees. A provision of the articles of incorporation, a provision of the bylaws or a resolution adopted by the board authorizing or imposing dues, assessments or fees does not, of itself, create liability for dues, assessments or fees. An express or implied agreement, consent or acquiescence by the member is necessary to create liability for dues, assessments or fees. A member is deemed to have agreed to the liability if there exists at the time the member becomes a member a provision of the articles of incorporation, a provision of the bylaws, a provision of the declaration of a condominium or a planned community or a resolution adopted by the board authorizing or imposing dues, assessments or fees.

B. A homebuyer may implicitly consent to liability for dues, assessments and fees.

C. Unless the provision authorizing dues expressly limits the amount of the dues, the amount and the member's liability are subject to increase or decrease.

10-3614. Creditor's action against member

A. No creditor of the corporation may bring a proceeding to reach the liability of a member to the corporation unless final judgment has been rendered in favor of the creditor against the corporation, and execution has been returned unsatisfied in whole or in part.

B. All creditors of the corporation, with or without reducing their claims to judgment, may intervene in any creditor's proceeding brought under subsection A to reach and apply unpaid amounts due the corporation. Any or all members who owe amounts to the corporation may be joined in that proceeding.

C. In any proceeding by a creditor under this section, the member shall pay any amount that is determined to be owed by the member to the corporation directly to the corporation and not to any creditor. The member is not liable directly or indirectly for any costs incurred by the creditor in the proceeding. If the member has paid the amount to the corporation, the liability of the member to the corporation for that amount is fully satisfied, the member is no longer a party to the proceeding and is immune from further proceedings under this section for the amount.

10-3620. Resignation

A. A member may resign at any time, except as set forth in or authorized by the articles of incorporation or bylaws.

B. The resignation of a member does not relieve the member from any obligations the member may have to the corporation as a result of obligations incurred or commitments made prior to resignation.

C. This section does not apply to corporations that are condominium associations or planned community associations.

10-3621. Termination, expulsion and suspension

A. No member of a corporation may be expelled or suspended, and no membership or memberships in such a corporation may be terminated or suspended, except pursuant to a procedure that is set forth in the articles of incorporation, bylaws or an agreement between the member and the corporation or a procedure that is otherwise appropriate.

B. For purposes of subsection A, a procedure is otherwise appropriate if either:

1. The following are provided:

   a) A written notice at least fifteen days before the expulsion, suspension or termination and the reasons therefor.

   b) An opportunity for the member to be heard, orally or in writing, at least five days before the effective date of the expulsion, suspension or termination by a person or persons authorized to decide that the proposed expulsion, termination or suspension should not take place.

2. It is fair and reasonable taking into consideration all of the relevant facts and circumstances.

C. Any written notice that is mailed shall be sent to the last address of the member shown on the corporation's records.

D. Any proceeding challenging an expulsion, suspension or termination, including a proceeding in which defective notice is alleged, shall begin within six months after the effective date of the expulsion, suspension or termination.

E. A member who has been expelled or suspended may be liable to the corporation for dues, assessments or fees as a result of obligations incurred or commitments made prior to expulsion or suspension.

F. This section does not apply to corporations organized primarily for religious purposes.

10-3701. Annual and regular meetings; exceptions

A. Unless otherwise provided in the articles of incorporation or bylaws, a corporation with members shall hold a membership meeting annually at a time stated in or fixed in accordance with the bylaws.

B. A corporation with members may hold regular membership meetings at the times stated in or fixed in accordance with the bylaws.

C. A corporation may hold annual and regular membership meetings in or out of this state at the place stated in or fixed in accordance with the bylaws. If no place is stated in or fixed in accordance with the bylaws, the corporation shall hold annual and regular meetings at the corporation's principal office.

D. At regular meetings the members shall consider and act on any matter raised and that is consistent with the notice requirements of section 10-3705.

E. The failure to hold an annual or regular meeting at a time stated in or fixed in accordance with a corporation's bylaws does not affect the validity of any corporate action.

F. Notwithstanding this chapter, a condominium association shall comply with title 33, chapter 9 and a planned community association shall comply with title 33, chapter 16 to the extent that this chapter is inconsistent with title 33, chapters 9 and 16.

10-3702. Special meeting

A. A corporation with members shall hold a special meeting of members either:

1. On the call of its board or of the person or persons authorized to do so by the articles or bylaws.

2. Except as provided in the articles of incorporation or bylaws of a corporation organized primarily for religious purposes, if the holders of at least ten per cent of the voting power of any corporation sign, date and deliver to any corporate officer one or more written demands for the meeting describing the purpose or purposes for which it is to be held.

170

B. The close of business on the thirtieth day before delivery of the demand or demands for a special meeting to any corporate officer is the record date for the purpose of determining whether the ten per cent requirement of subsection A of this section has been met.

C. A corporation may hold a special meeting of members in or out of this state at the place stated in or fixed in accordance with the bylaws. If no place is stated or fixed in accordance with the bylaws, the corporation shall hold special meetings at the corporation's principal office.

D. Unless otherwise provided in the articles of incorporation or bylaws, the corporation may conduct only those matters at a special meeting of members that are within the purpose or purposes described in the meeting notice required by section 10-3705.

10-3703. Court ordered meeting; costs; attorney fees

A. The court in the county where a corporation's principal office is located, or if the corporation has no principal office in this state, the court in the county where the corporation's known place of business is located, may summarily order a meeting to be held on application by any of the following:

  1. Any member, if an annual meeting was not held within fifteen months after its last annual meeting.

  2. Any member, if a regular meeting is not held within forty days after the date it was required to be held.

  3. A member who signed a demand for a special meeting that is valid under section 10-3702 or a person or persons entitled to call a special meeting, if either:

    a) Notice of the special meeting was not given within thirty days after the date that the demand was delivered to a corporate officer.

    b) The special meeting was not held in accordance with the notice.

B. The court may:

  1. Fix the time and place of the meeting.

  2. Specify a record date for determining members entitled to notice of and to vote at the meeting.

3. Prescribe the form and content of the meeting notice.

C. If the court orders a meeting, it may also order the corporation to pay the member's costs, including reasonable attorney fees, incurred to obtain the order.

10-3704. Action by written consent; definition

A. The members may approve any action that is required or permitted by chapters 24 through 40 of this title and that requires the members' approval without a meeting of members if the action is approved by members holding at least a majority of the voting power, unless the articles of incorporation, bylaws or chapters 24 through 40 of this title require a different amount of voting power. The action shall be evidenced by one or more written consents describing the action taken, signed by those members representing at least the requisite amount of the voting power, and delivered to the corporation for inclusion in the minutes or filing with the corporate records.

B. If not otherwise fixed under section 10-3703 or 10-3707, the record date for determining members entitled to take action without a meeting is the date the first member signs the consent under subsection A of this section.

C. The consent signed under this section has the effect of a meeting vote and may be described as such in any document.

D. Written notice of member approval pursuant to this section shall be given to all members who have not signed the written consent.

E. Unless otherwise specified in the consent or consents, the action is effective on the date that the consent or consents are signed by the last member whose signature results in the requisite amount of the voting power, except that if chapters 24 through 40 of this title require notice of proposed actions to members who are not entitled to vote in the action and the action is to be taken by unanimous consent of the members entitled to vote, the effective date is not before ten days after the corporation gives its members not entitled to vote written notice of the proposed action. The notice shall contain or be accompanied by the same material that under chapters 24 through 40 of this title would have been sent to members not entitled to vote in a notice of meeting at which the proposed action would have been submitted to the members for action.

F. Any member may revoke the member's consent by delivering a signed revocation of the consent to the president or secretary before the date that the consent or consents are signed by the last member whose signature results in the requisite amount of the voting power.

G. For the purposes of this section, "signature" includes an electronic signature as defined in section 44-7002.

10-3705. Notice of meeting

A. Except as provided in section 33-2208, a corporation shall notify members of the date, time and place of each annual, regular and special members' meeting at least ten days but not more than sixty days before the meeting date. Unless chapters 24 through 40 of this title or the articles of incorporation or bylaws require otherwise, the corporation shall give notice only to members entitled to vote at the meeting.

B. Unless chapters 24 through 40 of this title or the articles of incorporation or bylaws require otherwise, the notice of an annual or regular meeting does not require a description of the purpose or purposes for which the meeting is called.

C. Notice of a special meeting shall include a description of the purpose or purposes for which the meeting is called.

D. If not otherwise fixed under section 10-3703 or 10-3707, the record date for determining members entitled to notice of and to vote at an annual, regular or special members' meeting is the day before the effective date of the first notice to the members.

E. Unless the bylaws require otherwise, if an annual, regular or special members' meeting is adjourned to a different date, time or place, a notice of the new date, time or place is not required if the new date, time or place is announced at the meeting before adjournment. If a new record date for the adjourned meeting is or must be fixed under section 10-3707, the corporation shall give notice of the adjourned meeting pursuant to this section to persons who are members as of the new record date.

10-3706. Waiver of notice

A. A member may waive any notice required by chapters 24 through 40 of this title, the articles of incorporation or bylaws before or after the date and time stated in the notice. The waiver shall be in writing, be signed by the member entitled to the notice, and be delivered to the corporation for inclusion in the minutes or filing with the corporate records.

B. A member's attendance at a meeting:

    1. Waives objection to lack of notice or defective notice of the meeting, unless the member at the beginning of the meeting objects to holding the meeting or transacting business at the meeting.

    2. Waives objection to consideration of a particular matter at the meeting that is not within the purpose or purposes described in the meeting notice, unless the member objects to considering the matter at the time it is presented.

10-3707. Record date; determining members entitled to notice and vote

A. The bylaws of a corporation may fix or provide the manner of fixing a date as the record date for determining the members entitled to notice of a members' meeting. If the bylaws do not fix or provide for fixing that record date, the board may fix a future date as that record date. If that record date is not fixed, members at the close of business on the business day before the day on which notice is given, or if notice is waived, at the close of business on the business day before the day on which the meeting is held, are entitled to notice of the meeting.

B. The bylaws of a corporation may fix or provide the manner of fixing a date as the record date for determining the members entitled to vote at a members' meeting. If the bylaws do not fix or provide for fixing that record date, the board may fix a future date as that record date. If that record date is not fixed, members on the date of the meeting who are otherwise eligible to vote are entitled to vote at the meeting.

C. The bylaws may fix or provide the manner for determining a date as the record date for the purpose of determining the members entitled to exercise any rights in respect of any other lawful action. If the bylaws do not fix or provide for fixing that record date, the board may fix in advance that record date. If that record date is not fixed, members at the close of business on the day on which the board adopts the resolution relating to that record date, or the sixtieth day before the date of other action, whichever is later, are entitled to exercise those rights.

D. The record date fixed under this section shall not be more than seventy days before the meeting or action requiring a determination of members.

E. A determination of members entitled to notice of or to vote at a membership meeting is effective for any adjournment of the meeting, unless the board fixed a new date for determining the right to notice or the right to vote. The board shall fix a new date for determining the right to notice or the right to vote if the meeting is adjourned to a date that is more than seventy days after the record date for determining members entitled to notice of the original meeting.

F. If a court orders a meeting adjourned to another date, the original record date for notice of voting continues in effect.

10-3708. Action by written ballot

A. Unless prohibited or limited by the articles of incorporation or bylaws, any action that the corporation may take at any annual, regular or special meeting of members may be taken without a meeting if the corporation delivers a written ballot to every member entitled to vote on the matter.

B. A written ballot shall:

1. Set forth each proposed action.

2. Provide an opportunity to vote for or against each proposed action.

C. Approval by written ballot pursuant to this section is valid only if both:

1. The number of votes cast by ballot equals or exceeds the quorum required to be present at a meeting authorizing the action.

2. The number of approvals equals or exceeds the number of votes that would be required to approve the matter at a meeting at which the total number of votes cast was the same as the number of votes cast by ballot.

D. All solicitations for votes by written ballot shall:

1. Indicate the number of responses needed to meet the quorum requirements.

2. State the percentage of approvals necessary to approve each matter other than election of directors.

3. Specify the time by which a ballot must be delivered to the corporation in order to be counted, which time shall not be less than three days after the date that the corporation delivers the ballot.

E. Except as otherwise provided in the articles of incorporation or bylaws, a written ballot shall not be revoked.

10-3720. Members' list for meeting

A. After fixing a record date for a meeting, a corporation shall prepare an alphabetical list of the names of all of its members who are entitled to notice of the meeting. The list shall show the address and number of votes each member is entitled to vote at the meeting. The corporation shall prepare on a current basis through the time of the membership meeting another list of members, if any, who are entitled to vote at the meeting, but not entitled to notice of the meeting and the corporation shall prepare that list on the same basis and make it a part of the list of members.

B. For the purpose of communication with other members concerning the meeting the corporation shall make the list of members available for inspection by any member at the corporation's principal office or at another place identified in the meeting notice in the city where the meeting will be held. On written demand a member, a member's agent or a member's attorney may inspect and, subject to the limitations of section 10-11602, subsection C, and section 10-11605, may copy the list, during regular business hours and at the member's expense, during the period it is available for inspection.

C. The corporation shall make the list of members available at the meeting, and any member, a member's agent or a member's attorney may inspect the list at any time during the meeting or during any adjournment.

D. If the corporation refuses to allow a member, a member's agent or a member's attorney to inspect the list of members before or at the meeting or copy the list as permitted by subsection B of this section, the court in the county where a corporation's principal office is located, or if no principal office is located in this state, the court in the county where a corporation's known place of business is located, on application of the member, may summarily order the inspection or copying at the corporation's expense and may postpone the meeting for which the list was prepared until the inspection or copying is complete.

E. Refusal or failure to comply with this section does not affect the validity of any action taken at the meeting.

F. The articles of incorporation or bylaws of a corporation organized primarily for religious purposes may limit or abolish the rights of a member under this section to inspect and copy any corporate record.

10-3721. Voting entitlement generally

A. Unless the articles of incorporation or bylaws provide otherwise, each member is entitled to one vote on each matter voted on by the members. A member is entitled to vote only on those matters expressly provided in the articles of incorporation or bylaws.

B. Unless the articles of incorporation or bylaws or written agreement signed by the subject members and delivered to the corporation provide otherwise, if a membership stands of record in the names of two or more persons, those persons' acts with respect to voting shall have the following effect:

1. If only one votes, the act binds all.

2. If more than one votes, the vote shall be divided on a pro rata basis.

10-3722. Quorum requirements

Unless chapters 24 through 40 of this title or the articles of incorporation provide for a higher or lower quorum the bylaws may provide the number or percentage of members entitled to vote, present or represented by proxy, or the number or percentage of votes entitled to be cast by members present or represented by proxy, that shall constitute a quorum at a meeting of members. In the absence of that provision, members, present or represented by proxy, holding one-tenth of the votes entitled to be cast, shall constitute a quorum.

10-3723. Voting requirements

Unless chapters 24 through 40 of this title provide otherwise, the articles of incorporation or the bylaws require a greater vote or voting by class, if a quorum is present, the affirmative vote of the votes represented and voting, for which affirmative votes also constitute a majority of the required quorum, is the act of the members.

10-3724. Proxies

A. A member may vote the member's votes in person or by proxy.

B. Unless the articles of incorporation or bylaws prohibit or limit proxy voting, a member may appoint a proxy to vote or otherwise act for the member by signing an appointment form, either personally or by the member's attorney-in-fact.

C. An appointment of a proxy is effective on receipt by the secretary or other officer or agent authorized to tabulate votes. An appointment is valid for eleven months unless a different period is expressly provided in the appointment form.

D. An appointment of a proxy is revocable by the member unless the appointment form conspicuously states that it is irrevocable and the appointment is coupled with an interest. Appointments coupled with an interest include the appointment of any of the following:

   1. A pledgee.

   2. A person who purchased, agreed to purchase, holds an option to purchase or holds any other right to acquire the membership interest.

   3. A creditor of the corporation who extended or continued credit to the corporation under terms requiring the appointment.

   4. An employee of the corporation whose employment contract requires the appointment.

   5. A party to a voting agreement created pursuant to section 10-3731.

E. The death or incapacity of the member who appoints a proxy does not affect the right of the corporation to accept the proxy's authority unless the secretary or other officer or agent authorized to tabulate votes receives written notice of the death or incapacity before the proxy exercises authority under the appointment.

F. Appointment of a proxy is revoked by the person who appoints the proxy by either:

　1. Attending any meeting and voting in person.

　2. Signing and delivering to the secretary or other officer or agent authorized to tabulate proxy votes either a writing stating that the appointment of the proxy is revoked or a subsequent appointment form.

G. An appointment made irrevocable under subsection D of this section is revoked if the interest with which it is coupled is extinguished.

H. A transferee for value of a membership interest subject to an irrevocable appointment may revoke the appointment if the transferee did not know of its existence at the time that the transferee acquired the membership interest and the existence of the irrevocable appointment was not noted conspicuously on the transfer documents.

I. Subject to section 10-3727 and to any express limitation on the proxy's authority that appears on the face of the appointment form, a corporation may accept the proxy's vote or other action as that of the member making the appointment.

10-3725. Cumulative voting for directors

A. If the articles of incorporation or bylaws provide for cumulative voting by members, members may cumulate their votes for directors, by multiplying the number of votes the members are entitled to cast by the number of directors for whom they are entitled to vote and casting the product for a single candidate or by distributing the product among two or more candidates.

B. Cumulative voting is not authorized at a particular meeting unless either:

　1. The meeting notice or statement accompanying the notice states conspicuously that cumulative voting is authorized.

　2. A member who has the right to cumulate votes gives notice during the meeting and before the vote is taken of the

member's intent to cumulate votes during the meeting, and if one member gives this notice all other members in the same voting group participating in the election are entitled to cumulate their votes without giving further notice.

C. A director elected by cumulative voting may be removed by the members without cause if the requirements of section 10-3808 are met unless the votes cast against removal, or those members not consenting in writing or by ballot to the removal, would be sufficient to elect that director if voted cumulatively at an election at which the same total number of votes were cast or, if the action is taken by written consent or ballot, all memberships entitled to vote were voted and the entire number of directors authorized at the time of the director's most recent election were then being elected.

10-3726. Other methods of electing directors

A corporation may provide in its articles of incorporation or bylaws the process for election of directors by members or delegates by any of the following means:

1. On the basis of chapter or other organizational unit.

2. By region or other geographic unit.

3. By preferential voting.

4. By any other reasonable method.

10-3727. Corporation's acceptance of votes

A. If the name signed on a vote, consent, waiver or proxy appointment corresponds to the name of a member, the corporation if acting in good faith is entitled to accept the vote, consent, waiver or proxy appointment and give it effect as the act of the member.

B. If the name signed on a vote, consent, waiver or proxy appointment does not correspond to the record name of a member, the corporation if acting in good faith is entitled to accept the vote, consent, waiver or proxy appointment and give it effect as the act of the member if:

1. The member is an entity and the name signed purports to be that of an officer or agent of the entity.

2. The name signed purports to be that of an administrator, executor, guardian or conservator representing the member and, if the corporation requests, evidence of fiduciary status acceptable to the corporation has been presented with respect to the vote, consent, waiver or proxy appointment.

3. The name signed purports to be that of a receiver or trustee in bankruptcy of the member, and, if the corporation requests, evidence of this status acceptable to the corporation has been presented with respect to the vote, consent, waiver or proxy appointment.

4. The name signed purports to be that of a pledgee, beneficial owner or attorney-in-fact of the member and, if the corporation requests, evidence acceptable to the corporation of the signatory's authority to sign for the member has been presented with respect to the vote, consent, waiver or proxy appointment.

5. Two or more persons hold the membership as cotenants or fiduciaries and the name signed purports to be the name of at least one of the co-holders and the person signing appears to be acting on behalf of all the co-holders.

C. The corporation is entitled to reject a vote, consent, waiver or proxy appointment if the secretary or other officer or agent authorized to tabulate votes, acting in good faith, has reasonable basis for doubt about the validity of the signature on it or about the signatory's authority to sign for the member.

D. The corporation and its officer or agent who accepts or rejects a vote, consent, waiver or proxy appointment in good faith and in accordance with the standards of this section are not liable in damages to the member for the consequences of the acceptance or rejection.

E. Corporate action based on the acceptance or rejection of a vote, consent, waiver or proxy appointment under this section is valid unless a court of competent jurisdiction determines otherwise.

10-3801. Requirement for and duties of board

A. Each corporation shall have a board of directors.

B. All corporate powers shall be exercised by or under the authority of and the affairs of the corporation shall be managed under the direction of its board of directors, subject to any limitation set forth in the articles of incorporation.

C. The articles of incorporation may authorize one or more members, delegates or other persons to exercise some or all of the powers, which would otherwise be exercised by a board. To the extent so authorized the authorized person or persons shall have the duties and responsibilities of the directors, and the directors shall be relieved to that extent from those duties and responsibilities.

10-3802. Qualifications of directors

The articles of incorporation or bylaws may prescribe qualifications for directors. A director need not be a resident of this state or a member of the corporation unless the articles of incorporation or bylaws so prescribe.

10-3803. Number of directors

A. A board of directors shall consist of one or more individuals, with the number specified in or fixed in accordance with the articles of incorporation or bylaws.

B. The articles of incorporation or bylaws may establish a variable range for the size of the board of directors by fixing a minimum and maximum number of directors. If a variable range is established, the number of directors may be fixed or changed, from time to time, within the minimum and maximum, by the members or the board of directors.

10-3804. Election, designation and appointment of Directors

A. If the corporation has members, the members shall elect all the directors except the initial directors at the first annual meeting of members, and at each annual meeting after the first annual meeting, unless either:

   1. The terms of the directors are staggered pursuant to section 10-3806.

   2. The articles of incorporation or bylaws provide some other time or method of election.

3. The articles of incorporation or bylaws provide that some of the directors are appointed by some other person or some of the directors are designated.

B. If the corporation does not have members, all the directors except the initial directors shall be elected, appointed or designated as provided in the articles of incorporation or bylaws. If no method of designation or appointment is set forth in the articles of incorporation or bylaws, the board of directors shall elect the directors other than the initial directors.

10-3805. Terms of directors generally

A. The terms of the initial directors of a corporation expire at the first election, appointment or designation of directors as provided in section 10-3804.

B. The articles of incorporation or bylaws shall specify the terms of directors. In the absence of any term specified in the articles of incorporation or bylaws, the term of each director is one year. Unless otherwise provided in the articles of incorporation or bylaws, directors may be elected for successive terms.

C. A decrease in the number of directors or term of office does not shorten the term of any incumbent director.

D. Except as provided in the articles of incorporation or bylaws:

1. The term of a director elected to fill a vacancy in the office of a director elected by members expires at the next election of directors by members.

2. The term of a director elected to fill any other vacancy expires at the end of the unexpired term that the director is filling.

E. Despite the expiration of a director's term, a director shall continue to hold office until the director's successor is elected, designated or appointed and qualifies, until the director's resignation or removal or until there is a decrease in the number of directors.

10-3806. Staggered terms for directors

The articles of incorporation or bylaws may provide for staggering the directors' terms of office by dividing the total number of directors into two or more groups. The terms of office of the several groups need not be uniform.

10-3807. Resignation of directors

A. A director may resign at any time by delivering written notice to the board of directors, its presiding officer or the corporation.

B. A resignation is effective when the notice is delivered unless the notice specifies a later effective date or event. If a resignation is made effective at a later date, the board may fill the pending vacancy before the effective date if the board provides that the successor does not take office until the effective date.

10-3808. Removal of directors elected by members or directors

A. A director may be removed from office pursuant to any procedure provided in the articles of incorporation or bylaws.

B. If the articles of incorporation or bylaws do not provide a procedure for removal of a director from office:

1. The members may remove one or more directors elected by them with or without cause unless the articles of incorporation provide that directors may be removed only for cause.

2. If a director is elected by a class, chapter, region or other organizational or geographic unit or grouping only the members of that class, chapter, region, unit or grouping may participate in the vote to remove the director.

3. Except as provided in paragraph 9, a director may be removed under paragraph 1 or 2 only if the number of votes cast to remove the director would be sufficient to elect the director at a meeting to elect directors.

4. If cumulative voting is authorized, a director may not be removed if the number of votes, or if the director was elected by a class, chapter, region, unit or grouping of members, the number of votes of that class, chapter, region, unit or grouping, sufficient to elect the director under cumulative voting is voted against the director's removal.

5. A director elected by members may be removed by the members at a meeting by written consent or by written ballot of the members authorized to vote on such removal. If the

removal is to occur at a meeting, the meeting notice shall state that the purpose or one of the purposes of the meeting is removal of the director.

6. In computing whether a director is protected from removal under paragraphs 2 through 4, it is assumed that the votes against removal are cast in an election for the number of directors of the class to which the director to be removed belonged on the date of that director's election.

7. An entire board of directors may be removed under paragraphs 1 through 5.

8. Except as provided in subsection C, a director elected by the board may be removed with or without cause by the vote of two-thirds of the directors then in office or any greater number as is set forth in the articles of incorporation or bylaws.

9. If, at the beginning of a director's term on the board of directors, the articles of incorporation or bylaws provide that the director may be removed for missing a specified number of meetings of the board of directors, the board of directors may remove the director for failing to attend the specified number of meetings. The director may be removed only if a majority of the directors then in office vote for the removal.

C. Notwithstanding subsection B, paragraph 8, a director elected by the board to fill the vacancy of a director elected by the members may be removed with or without cause by the members, but not by the board of directors.

10-3809. Removal of designated or appointed directors

A. A designated director may be removed by an amendment to the articles of incorporation or bylaws deleting or changing the designation.

B. Except as otherwise provided in the articles of incorporation or bylaws, an appointed director may be removed with or without cause by the person appointing the director. The person removing the director shall give written notice of the removal to the director and either the board of directors, its presiding officer or the corporation. A removal is effective when the notice is delivered unless the notice specifies a later effective date or event.

10-3810. Removal of directors by judicial proceeding

A. The court in the county where a corporation's known place of business or, if none in this state, its statutory agent is located may remove a director of the corporation from office in a proceeding commenced either by the corporation or by its members holding at least twenty-five per cent of the voting power of any class, if the court finds that both:

　1. The director engaged in fraudulent conduct or intentional criminal conduct with respect to the corporation.

　2. Removal is in the best interests of the corporation.

B. The court that removes a director may bar the director from serving on the board for a period prescribed by the court, but in no event may the period exceed five years.

C. If members commence a proceeding under subsection A, they shall make the corporation a party defendant, unless the corporation elects to become a party plaintiff.

D. The articles of incorporation or bylaws of a corporation organized for religious purposes may limit or prohibit the application of this section.

10-3811. Vacancy on board

A. Unless the articles of incorporation or bylaws provide otherwise, and except as provided in subsections B and C of this section, if a vacancy occurs on a board of directors, including a vacancy resulting from an increase in the number of directors, either:

　1. The members, if any, may fill the vacancy.

　2. The board of directors may fill the vacancy.

　3. If the directors remaining in office constitute fewer than a quorum of the board of directors, they may fill the vacancy by the affirmative vote of a majority of all the directors remaining in office.

B. Unless the articles of incorporation or bylaws provide otherwise, if the vacant office was held by a director elected by a class, chapter, region or other organizational or geographic unit or grouping, only members of the class, chapter, region, unit or grouping are entitled to vote to fill the vacancy if it is filled by the members.

C. Unless the articles of incorporation or bylaws provide otherwise, if a vacant office was held by an appointed director, only the person who appointed the director may fill the vacancy.

D. If a vacant office was held by a designated director, the vacancy shall be filled as provided in the articles of incorporation or bylaws. In the absence of an applicable article or bylaw provision, the vacancy may not be filled by the board.

E. A vacancy that will occur at a specific later date by reason of a resignation effective at a later date under section 10-3807, subsection B or otherwise may be filled before the vacancy occurs, but the new director may not take office until the vacancy occurs.

F. If at any time by reason of death or resignation or other cause a corporation has no directors in office, any officer or any member may call a special meeting of members.

10-3812. Compensation of directors

Unless the articles of incorporation or bylaws provide otherwise, the board of directors may fix the compensation of directors.

10-3820. Regular and special meetings

A. If the time and place of a directors' meeting is fixed by the bylaws or the board of directors, the meeting is a regular meeting. All other meetings are special meetings.

B. A board of directors may hold regular or special meetings in or out of this state.

C. Unless the articles of incorporation or bylaws provide otherwise, the board of directors may permit any or all directors to participate in a regular or special meeting by or conduct the meeting through the use of any means of communication by which all directors participating may simultaneously hear each other during the meeting. A director participating in a meeting by this means is deemed to be present in person at the meeting.

10-3821. Action without meeting

A. Unless the articles of incorporation or bylaws provide otherwise, action required or permitted by chapters 24 through 40 of this title to be taken at a directors' meeting may be taken without a meeting if the action is taken by all of the directors. The action must be evidenced by one or more written consents describing the action taken, signed by each director and included in the minutes filed with the corporate records reflecting the action taken.

B. Action taken under this section is effective when the last director signs the consent, unless the consent specifies a different effective date.

C. The consent signed under this section has the effect of a meeting vote and may be described as such in any document.

D. Any director may revoke a consent by delivering a signed revocation of the consent to the president or secretary before the date the last director signs the consent.

E. For the purposes of this section, a consent may be signed using an electronic signature as defined in section 44-7002.

10-3822. Call and notice of meetings

A. Unless the articles of incorporation, bylaws or subsection C of this section provide otherwise, regular meetings of the board of directors may be held without notice of the date, time, place or purpose of the meeting.

B. Unless the articles of incorporation, bylaws or subsection C of this section provide otherwise, special meetings of the board of directors shall be preceded by at least two days' notice of the date, time and place of the meeting. The notice need not describe the purpose of the special meeting unless required by the articles of incorporation or bylaws.

C. In corporations without members any board action to remove a director or to approve a matter that would require approval by the members if the corporation had members is not valid unless each director is given at least two days' written notice that the matter will be voted on at a directors' meeting or unless notice is waived pursuant to section 10-3823.

D. Unless the articles of incorporation or bylaws provide otherwise, the presiding officer of the board of directors, the president or twenty per cent of the directors then in office may call and give notice of a meeting of the board.

10-3823. Waiver of notice

A. A director may waive any notice required by chapters 24 through 40 of this title, the articles of incorporation or bylaws before or after the date and time stated in the notice. Except as provided in subsection B of this section, the waiver shall be in writing and signed by the director entitled to the notice, or by electronic mail and filed with the minutes or corporate records.

B. A director's attendance at or participation in a meeting waives any required notice to the director of the meeting unless the director at the beginning of the meeting or promptly on the director's arrival at the meeting objects to holding the meeting or transacting business at the meeting and does not thereafter vote for or assent to action taken at the meeting.

C. For the purposes of this section, a waiver may be signed using an electronic signature as defined in section 44-7002.

10-3824. Quorum and voting

A. Unless the articles of incorporation or bylaws require a different number, a quorum of a board of directors consists of either:

1. A majority of the fixed number of directors if the corporation has a fixed board size.

2. A majority of the number of directors prescribed, or if no number is prescribed, the number in office immediately before the meeting begins, if the corporation has a variable range size board.

B. The articles of incorporation or bylaws may authorize a quorum of a board of directors to consist of at least one-third of the fixed or prescribed number of directors determined under subsection A.

C. The articles of incorporation or bylaws may specify that, if a quorum is present when a meeting is convened, the quorum shall be deemed to exist until the meeting is adjourned, notwithstanding the departure of one or more directors.

D. If a quorum is present when a vote is taken, the affirmative vote of a majority of directors present is the act of the board of directors unless the articles of incorporation or bylaws require the vote of a greater number of directors.

E. A director who is present at a meeting of the board of directors or a committee of the board of directors when corporate action is taken is deemed to have assented to the action taken unless either:

  1. The director objects at the beginning of the meeting or promptly on the director's arrival to holding it or transacting business at the meeting.

  2. The director's dissent or abstention from the action taken is entered in the minutes of the meeting.

  3. The director delivers written notice of the director's dissent or abstention to the presiding officer of the meeting before its adjournment or to the corporation before 5:00 p.m. on the next business day after the meeting.

F. The right of dissent or abstention is not available to a director who votes in favor of the action taken.

G. The articles of incorporation or bylaws may authorize a director to vote in person or by proxy. The following provisions apply to voting by proxy:

  1. A director may appoint a proxy to vote or otherwise act for the director by signing an appointment form, either personally or by the director's attorney-in-fact. The appointment does not relieve the director of liability for acts or omissions imposed by law on directors.

  2. An appointment of a proxy is effective when received by the secretary. An appointment is valid for one month unless a different period is expressly provided in the appointment form.

  3. An appointment of a proxy is revocable by the director.

  4. The death or incapacity of the director appointing a proxy does not affect the right of the corporation to accept the proxy's authority unless written notice of the death or incapacity is received by the secretary before the proxy exercises its authority under the appointment.

  5. Subject to any express limitation on the proxy's authority appearing on the face of the appointment form, a corporation is entitled to accept the proxy's vote or other action as of the shareholder making the appointment.

10-3825. Committees of the board

A. Unless the articles of incorporation or bylaws provide otherwise, the board of directors may create one or more committees and appoint members of the board of directors to serve on them. Each committee shall have one or more members, and each member of a committee shall serve at the pleasure of the board of directors.

B. The creation of a committee and appointment of members of the board of directors to it must be approved by the greater of:

1. A majority of all the directors in office when the action is taken.

2. The number of directors required by the articles of incorporation or bylaws to take action under section 10-3824.

C. Sections 10-3820 through 10-3824 governing meetings, action without meetings and notice, waiver of notice, quorum and voting requirements of the board of directors also apply to committees and their members.

D. Subject to the limitations set forth in subsection E of this section, each committee of the board may exercise the authority of the board of directors under section 10-3801 to the extent specified by the board of directors or in the articles of incorporation or bylaws.

E. A committee shall not take any of the following actions:

1. Authorize distributions.

2. Approve or recommend to members any action that requires the members' approval under this chapter.

3. Fill vacancies on the board of directors or on any of its committees.

4. Adopt, amend or repeal bylaws.

5. Fix the compensation of directors for serving on the board of directors or any committee of the board of directors.

F. The creation of, delegation of authority to or action by a committee does not alone constitute compliance by a director with the standards of conduct described in section 10-3830.

G. The board of directors may designate one or more directors as alternate members of any committee who may replace any absent member at any meeting of the committee.

10-3830. General standards for directors

A. A director's duties, including duties as a member of a committee, shall be discharged:

   1. In good faith.

   2. With the care an ordinarily prudent person in a like position would exercise under similar circumstances.

   3. In a manner the director reasonably believes to be in the best interests of the corporation.

B. In discharging duties, a director is entitled to rely on information, opinions, reports or statements, including financial statements and other financial data, if prepared or presented by any of the following:

   1. One or more officers or employees of the corporation whom the director reasonably believes are reliable and competent in the matters presented.

   2. Legal counsel, public accountants or other person as to matters the director reasonably believes are within the person's professional or expert competence.

   3. A committee of or appointed by the board of directors of which the director is not a member if the director reasonably believes the committee merits confidence.

   4. In the case of corporations organized for religious purposes, religious authorities and ministers, priests, rabbis or other persons whose position or duties in the religious organization the director believes justify reliance and confidence and whom the director believes to be reliable and competent in the matters presented.

C. A director is not acting in good faith if the director has knowledge concerning the matter in question that makes reliance otherwise permitted by subsection B unwarranted.

D. A director is not liable for any action taken as a director or any failure to take any action if the director's duties were performed in compliance with this section. In any proceeding commenced under this section or any other provision of this chapter, a director has all of the defenses and presumptions ordinarily available to a director. A director is presumed in all cases to have acted, failed to act or otherwise discharged such director's duties in accordance with subsection A. The burden is on the party challenging a director's action, failure to act or other discharge of duties to establish by clear and convincing evidence facts rebutting the presumption.

E. A director shall not be deemed to be a trustee with respect to the corporation or with respect to any property held or administered by the corporation, including property that may be subject to restrictions imposed by the donor or transferor of that property.

10-3833. Liability for unlawful distributions

A. A director who votes for or assents to a distribution made in violation of sections 10-11301 and 10-11302 or the articles of incorporation is personally liable to the corporation for the amount of the distribution that exceeds what could have been distributed without violating sections 10-11301 and 10-11302 or the articles of incorporation if it is established that the director's duties were not performed in compliance with section 10-3830.

B. A director of a corporation who is present at a meeting of its board of directors at which action on any distribution in violation of section 10-11301 is taken is presumed to have assented to the action taken unless his dissent is entered in the minutes of the meeting or unless he files his written dissent to the action with the secretary of the meeting before the adjournment of the meeting or forwards the dissent by registered or certified mail to the secretary of the corporation before 5:00 p.m. of the next business day after the adjournment of the meeting. The right to dissent does not apply to a director who voted in favor of the action.

C. A director who is held liable under subsection A of this section for an unlawful distribution is entitled to contribution from:

1. Every other director who could be held liable under subsection A of this section for the unlawful distribution.

2. Each person who received an unlawful distribution for the amount of the distribution whether or not the person receiving the distribution knew it was made in violation of sections 10-11301 and 10-11302 or the articles of incorporation.

D. A proceeding under this section is barred unless it is commenced within two years after the date on which the distribution is made.

10-3840. Officers

A. A corporation shall have the officers described in its articles of incorporation or bylaws or appointed by the board of directors in accordance with the articles of incorporation or bylaws.

B. A duly appointed officer may appoint one or more officers or assistant officers if authorized by the bylaws or the board of directors.

C. The bylaws or the board of directors shall delegate to one of the officers responsibility for preparing minutes of the directors' and members' meetings and for authenticating records of the corporation.

D. The same individual may simultaneously hold more than one office in a corporation.

10-3841. Duties and authority of officers

Each officer has the authority and shall perform the duties set forth in the bylaws or, to the extent consistent with the bylaws, the duties and authority prescribed by the board of directors or by direction of an officer authorized by the board of directors to prescribe the duties and authority of other officers.

10-3842. Standards of conduct for officers

A. If an officer has discretionary authority with respect to any duties, an officer's duties shall be discharged under that authority:

1. In good faith.

2. With the care an ordinarily prudent person in a like position would exercise under similar circumstances.

3. In a manner the officer reasonably believes to be in the best interests of the corporation.

B. In discharging duties, an officer is entitled to rely on information, opinions, reports or statements, including financial statements and other financial data, if prepared or presented by either:

1. One or more officers or employees of the corporation whom the officer reasonably believes to be reliable and competent in the matters presented.

2. Legal counsel, public accountants or other persons as to matters the officer reasonably believes are within the person's professional or expert competence.

3. In the case of corporations organized for religious purposes, religious authorities and ministers, priests, rabbis or other persons whose position or duties in the religious organization the officer believes justify reliance and confidence and who the officer believes to be reliable and competent in the matters presented.

C. An officer is not acting in good faith if the officer has knowledge concerning the matter in question that makes reliance otherwise permitted by subsection B unwarranted.

D. An officer is not liable for any action taken as an officer or any failure to take any action if the officer's duties were performed in compliance with this section. In any proceeding commenced under this section or any other provision of this chapter, an officer has all of the defenses and presumptions ordinarily available to an officer. An officer is presumed in all cases to have acted, failed to act or otherwise discharged such officer's duties in accordance with subsection A. The burden is on the party challenging an officer's action, failure to act or other discharge of duties to establish by clear and convincing evidence facts rebutting the presumption.

10-3843. Resignation and removal of officers

A. An officer may resign at any time by delivering notice to the corporation. A resignation is effective when the notice is delivered unless the notice specifies a later effective date or event. If a resignation is made effective at a later date or event and the corporation accepts the later effective date, its board of directors may fill the pending vacancy before the effective date if the board of directors provides that the successor does not take office until the effective date.

B. A board of directors may remove any officer at any time with or without cause.

10-3844. Contract rights of officers

A. The appointment of an officer does not itself create contract rights.

B. An officer's removal does not affect the officer's contract rights, if any, with the corporation. An officer's resignation does not affect the corporation's contract rights, if any, with the officer.

10-3845. Officers' authority to execute documents

Any contract or other instrument in writing executed or entered into between a corporation and any other person is not invalidated as to the corporation by any lack of authority of the signing officers in the absence of actual knowledge on the part of the other person that the signing officers had no authority to execute the contract or other instrument if it is signed by two individuals who are either:

1. Both the presiding officer of the board of directors and the president.

2. Either the presiding officer of the board of directors or the president, and one of the following:

   a) A vice-president.

   b) The secretary.

   c) The treasurer.

   d) The executive director.

10-3850. Definitions

In this article, unless the context otherwise requires:

1. "Corporation" includes any domestic or foreign predecessor entity of a corporation in a merger or other transaction in which the predecessor's existence ceased upon consummation of the transaction.

2. "Director" means an individual who is or was a director of a corporation or an individual who, while a director of a corporation, is or was serving at the corporation's request as a director, officer, partner, trustee, employee or agent of another foreign or domestic corporation, partnership, joint venture, trust, employee benefit plan or other entity. A director is considered to be serving an employee benefit plan at the corporation's request if the director's duties to the corporation also impose duties on or otherwise involve

services by the director to the plan or to participants in or beneficiaries of the plan. Director includes the estate or personal representative of a director and includes ex officio members of the board.

3. "Expenses" include attorney fees and other costs and expenses reasonably related to a proceeding.

4. "Liability" means the obligation to pay a judgment, settlement, penalty or fine, including an excise tax assessed with respect to an employee benefit plan, or reasonable expenses actually incurred with respect to a proceeding and includes obligations and expenses that have not yet been paid by the indemnified persons but that have been or may be incurred.

5. "Officer" means an individual who is or was an officer of a corporation or an individual who, while an officer of a corporation, is or was serving at the corporation's request as a director, officer, partner, trustee, employee or agent of another foreign or domestic corporation, partnership, joint venture, trust, employee benefit plan or other entity. An officer is considered to be serving an employee benefit plan at the corporation's request if the officer's duties to the corporation also impose duties on or otherwise involve services by the officer to the plan or to participants in or beneficiaries of the plan. Officer includes the estate or personal representative of an officer.

6. "Official capacity" means if used with respect to a director, the office of director in a corporation and, if used with respect to an officer as contemplated in section 10-3856, the office in a corporation held by the officer. Official capacity does not include service for any other foreign or domestic corporation or any partnership, joint venture, trust, employee benefit plan, or other entity.

7. "Outside director" means a director who, when serving as a director, is not or was not a compensated officer, employee or member holding more than ten per cent of the voting power of the corporation or any affiliate of the corporation or an officer, employee or holder of more than ten per cent of the voting power of such a member or any affiliate of that member.

8. "Party" includes an individual who was, is or is threatened to be made a named defendant or respondent in a proceeding.

9. "Proceeding" means any threatened, pending or completed action, suit or proceeding, whether civil, criminal, administrative or investigative and whether formal or informal.

10-3851. Authority to indemnify

A. Except as provided in subsection D of this section, a corporation may indemnify an individual made a party to a proceeding because either:

1. The individual is or was a director against liability incurred in the proceeding if all of the following conditions exist:

   a) The individual's conduct was in good faith.

   b) The individual reasonably believed:

      i) In the case of conduct in an official capacity with the corporation, that the conduct was in its best interests.

      ii) In all other cases, that the conduct was at least not opposed to its best interests.

      (c) In the case of any criminal proceedings, the individual had no reasonable cause to believe the conduct was unlawful.

2. The director engaged in conduct for which broader indemnification has been made permissible or obligatory under a provision of the articles of incorporation pursuant to section 10-3202, subsection B, paragraph 2.

B. A director's conduct with respect to an employee benefit plan for a purpose the director reasonably believed to be in the interests of the participants in and beneficiaries of the plan is conduct that satisfies the requirement of subsection A, paragraph 1, subdivision (a) of this section.

C. The termination of a proceeding by judgment, order, settlement or conviction or on a plea of no contest or its equivalent is not of itself determinative that the director did not meet the standard of conduct described in this section.

D. A corporation may not indemnify a director under this section either:

1. In connection with a proceeding by or in the right of the corporation in which the director was adjudged liable to the corporation.

2. In connection with any other proceeding charging improper personal benefit to the director, whether or not involving action in the director's official capacity, in which the director was adjudged liable on the basis that personal benefit was improperly received by the director.

E. Indemnification permitted under this section in connection with a proceeding by or in the right of the corporation is limited to reasonable expenses incurred in connection with the proceeding.

10-3852. Mandatory indemnification

A. Unless limited by its articles of incorporation, a corporation shall indemnify a director who was the prevailing party, on the merits or otherwise, in the defense of any proceeding to which the director was a party because the director is or was a director of the corporation against reasonable expenses incurred by the director in connection with the proceeding.

B. Unless limited by its articles of incorporation, section 10-851, subsection D or subsection C of this section, a corporation shall indemnify an outside director against liability. Unless limited by its articles of incorporation or subsection C of this section, a corporation shall pay an outside director's expenses in advance of a final disposition of a proceeding, if the director furnishes the corporation with a written affirmation of the director's good faith belief that the director has met the standard of conduct described in section 10-851, subsection A and the director furnishes the corporation with a written undertaking executed personally, or on the director's behalf, to repay the advance if it is ultimately determined that the director did not meet the standard of conduct. The undertaking required by this subsection is an unlimited general obligation of the director but need not be secured and shall be accepted without reference to the director's financial ability to make repayment.

C. A corporation shall not provide the indemnification or advancement of expenses described in subsection B of this section if a court of competent jurisdiction has determined before payment that the outside director failed to meet the standards described in section 10-851, subsection A, and a court of competent jurisdiction does not otherwise authorize payment under section 10-854. A corporation shall not delay payment of indemnification or expenses under subsection B of this section for more than sixty days after a request is made unless ordered to do so by a court of competent jurisdiction.

10-3853. Advance for expenses

A. A corporation may pay for or reimburse the reasonable expenses incurred by a director who is a party to a proceeding in advance of final disposition of the proceeding if both of the following conditions exist:

1. The director furnishes to the corporation a written affirmation of the director's good faith belief that the director has met the standard of conduct described in section 10-3851 or that the proceeding involves conduct for which liability has been eliminated under a provision of the articles of incorporation pursuant to section 10-3202, subsection B, paragraph 1.

2. The director furnishes the corporation with a written undertaking, executed personally or on the director's behalf, to repay the advance if the director is not entitled to mandatory indemnification under section 10-3852 and it is ultimately determined that the director did not meet the standard of conduct.

B. The undertaking required by subsection A, paragraph 2 of this section is an unlimited general obligation of the director but need not be secured and may be accepted without reference to financial ability to make repayment.

C. Authorizations of payments under this section shall be made in a manner consistent with section 10-3830 or 10-3842.

D. This section does not apply to advancement of expenses to or for the benefit of an outside director. Advances to outside directors shall be made pursuant to section 10-3852.

10-3854. Court ordered indemnification

Unless a corporation's articles of incorporation provide otherwise, a director of the corporation who is a party to a proceeding may apply for indemnification or an advance for expenses to the court conducting the proceeding or to another court of competent jurisdiction. On receipt of an application, the court after giving any notice the court considers necessary may order indemnification advances for expenses if it determines either:

1. The director is entitled to mandatory indemnification under section 10-3852, in which case the court shall also order the corporation to pay the director's reasonable expenses incurred to obtain court ordered indemnification.

2. The director is fairly and reasonably entitled to indemnification in view of all the relevant circumstances, whether or not the director met the standard of conduct set forth in section 10-3851 or was adjudged liable as described in section 10-3851, subsection D, but if the director was adjudged liable under section 10-3851, subsection D, indemnification is limited to reasonable expenses incurred.

10-3855. Determination and authorization of indemnification

A. A corporation may not indemnify a director under section 10-3851 unless authorized in the specific case after a determination has been made that indemnification of the director is permissible in the circumstances because the director has met the standard of conduct set forth in section 10-3851.

B. The determination shall be made either:

1. By the board of directors by a majority vote of the directors not at the time parties to the proceeding.

2. By special legal counsel:

   a) Selected by majority vote of the disinterested directors.

   b) If there are no disinterested directors, selected by majority vote of the board of directors.

3. By the members, but directors who are at thetime parties to the proceeding may not vote on the determination.

C. Neither special legal counsel nor any member has any liability whatsoever for a determination made pursuant to this section. In voting pursuant to subsection B of this section, directors shall discharge their duty in accordance with section 10-3830.

D. Authorization of indemnification and evaluation as to reasonableness of expenses shall be made in the same manner as the determination that indemnification is permissible, except that if the determination is made by special legal counsel, authorization of indemnification and evaluation as to reasonableness of expenses shall be made by those entitled under subsection B, paragraph 2 of this section to select counsel.

10-3856. Indemnification of officers

A. A corporation may indemnify and advance expenses under this article to an officer of the corporation who is a party to a proceeding because the individual is or was an officer of the corporation as follows:

1. To the same extent as a director.

2. If the individual is an officer but not a director, to the further extent as may be provided by the articles of incorporation, the bylaws, a resolution of the board of directors, or contract except for:

   a) Liability in connection with a proceeding by or in the right of the corporation other than for reasonable expenses incurred in connection with the proceeding.

   b) Liability arising out of conduct that constitutes:

      i) Receipt by the officer of a financial benefit to which the officer is not entitled.

      ii) An intentional infliction of harm on the corporation or the members.

      iii) An intentional violation of criminal law.

B. Subsection A, paragraph 2 of this section applies to an officer who is also director if the basis on which the officer is made a party to the proceeding is an act or omission solely as an officer.

C. An officer of a corporation who is not a director is entitled to mandatory indemnification under section 10-3852, subsection A and may apply to a court under section 10-3854 for indemnification or an advance for expenses, in each case to the same extent to which a director is entitled to indemnification or advance for expenses under those sections.

10-3857. Insurance

A corporation may purchase and maintain insurance on behalf of an individual who is or was a director or officer of the corporation or who, while a director or officer of the corporation, is or was serving at the request of the corporation as a director, officer, partner, trustee, employee or agent of another foreign or domestic corporation, partnership, joint venture, trust, employee benefit plan or other entity, against liability asserted against or incurred by the individual in that capacity or arising from the individual's status as a director or officer, whether or not the corporation would have power to indemnify or advance expenses to the person against the same liability under this article.

10-3858. Application of article

A. A provision treating a corporation's indemnification of or advance for expenses to directors that is contained in its articles of incorporation, bylaws, a resolution of its members or board of directors or a contract or otherwise is valid only if and to the extent the provision is consistent with this article. If the articles of incorporation limit indemnification or advances for expenses, indemnification and advances for expenses are valid only to the extent consistent with the articles of incorporation.

B. This article does not limit a corporation's power to pay or reimburse expenses incurred by a director in connection with the director's appearance as a witness in a proceeding at a time when the director has not been made a named defendant or respondent to the proceeding.

C. This article does not limit a corporation's power to indemnify, advance expenses or maintain insurance on behalf of an employee or agent.

10-3860. Definitions

In this article, unless the context otherwise requires:

1. "Conflicting interest" with respect to a corporation means the interest a director of the corporation has respecting a transaction effected or proposed to be effected by the

corporation, by a subsidiary of the corporation or by any other entity in which the corporation has a controlling interest if either:

a) Whether or not the transaction is brought before the board of directors of the corporation for action, the director knows at the time of commitment that the director or a related person either:

   i) Is a party to the transaction.

   ii) Has a beneficial financial interest in or is so closely linked to the transaction and of such financial significance to the director or a related person that the interest would reasonably be expected to exert an influence on the director's judgment if he were called on to vote on the transaction.

b) The transaction is brought or is of such character and significance to the corporation that it would in the normal course be brought before the board of directors of the corporation for action, and the director knows at the time of commitment that any of the following persons is either a party to the transaction or has a beneficial financial interest in or is so closely linked to the transaction and of such financial significance to the person that the interest would reasonably be expected to exert an influence on the director's judgment if the director were called on to vote on the transaction:

   i) An entity, other than the corporation, of which the director is a director, general partner, agent or employee.

   ii) A person that controls one or more of the entities specified in item of this subdivision or an entity that is controlled by or is under common control with one or more of the entities specified in item

   iii) An individual who is a general partner, principal or employer of the director.

2. "Director's conflicting interest transaction" with respect to a corporation means a transaction effected or proposed to be effected by the corporation, by a subsidiary of the corporation or by any other entity in which the corporation

has a controlling interest respecting which a director of the corporation has a conflicting interest.

3. "Related person" of a director means either:

   a) The spouse, or a parent or sibling of the spouse, of the director, a child, grandchild, sibling, parent or spouse of a child, grandchild, sibling or parent, of the director, an individual having the same home as the director or a trust or estate of which an individual specified in this subdivision is a substantial beneficiary.

   b) A trust, estate, incompetent, conservatee or minor of which the director is a fiduciary.

4. "Required disclosure" means disclosure by the director who has a conflicting interest of both:

   a) The existence and nature of the conflicting interest.

   b) All facts known to the director respecting the subject matter of the transaction that an ordinarily prudent person would reasonably believe to be material to a judgment about whether or not to proceed with the transaction.

5. "Time of commitment" respecting a transaction means the time when the transaction is consummated or, if made pursuant to contract, the time when the corporation, or its subsidiary or the entity in which it has a controlling interest, becomes contractually obligated so that its unilateral withdrawal from the transaction would entail significant loss, liability or other damage.

10-3861. Judicial action

A. A transaction that is effected or proposed to be effected by a corporation, or by a subsidiary of the corporation or any other entity in which the corporation has a controlling interest, and that is not a director's conflicting interest transaction shall not be enjoined, be set aside or give rise to an award of damages or other sanctions in a proceeding by a member or by or in the right of the corporation, because a director of the corporation, or any person with whom or with which the director has a personal, economic or other association, has an interest in the transaction.

B. A director's conflicting interest transaction shall not be enjoined, be set aside or give rise to an award of damages or other sanctions in a proceeding by a member by or in the right of the corporation, because the director, or any person with whom or with which the director has a personal, economic or other association, has an interest in the transaction, if either:

1. Directors' action respecting the transaction was taken at any time in compliance with section 10-3862.

2. Members' action respecting the transaction was taken at any time in compliance with section 10-3863.

3. The transaction, judged according to the circumstances at the time of commitment, is established to have been fair to the corporation.

C. Any person seeking to have a director's conflicting interest transaction enjoined, set aside or give rise to an award of damages or other sanctions shall first prove by clear and convincing evidence that subsection B of this section is not applicable.

10-3862. Directors' action; definition

A. Directors' action respecting a transaction is effective for purposes of section 10-3861, subsection B, paragraph 1 if the transaction received the affirmative vote of a majority, but at least two, of those qualified directors on the board of directors or on a duly empowered committee of the board who voted on the transaction after either required disclosure to them, to the extent the information was not known by them, or compliance with subsection B of this section. Action by a committee is effective under this section only if both:

1. All of its members are qualified directors.

2. Members are either all of the qualified directors on the board or are appointed by the affirmative vote of a majority of the qualified directors or the board.

B. If a director has a conflicting interest regarding a transaction but neither the director nor a related person of the director specified in section 10-3860, paragraph 3, subdivision (a) is a party to the transaction and if the director has a duty under law or professional canon or a duty of confidentiality to another person, respecting information relating to the transaction such that the director may not make the disclosure described in section 10-

3860, paragraph 4, subdivision (b), disclosure is sufficient for purposes of subsection A of this section if the director both:

1. Discloses to the directors voting on the transaction the existence and nature of the conflicting interest and informs them of the character and limitations imposed by that duty before their vote on the transaction.

2. Plays no part, directly or indirectly, in their deliberations or vote.

C. A majority, but at least two, of all of the qualified directors on the board of directors or on the committee is a quorum for purposes of action that complies with this section. Directors' action that otherwise complies with this section is not affected by the presence or vote of a director who is not a qualified director.

D. For purposes of this section, "qualified director" means, with respect to a director's conflicting transaction, any director who does not have either:

1. A conflicting interest respecting the transaction.

2. A familial, financial, professional or employment relationship with a second director who does have a conflicting interest respecting the transaction, which relationship would, in the circumstances, reasonably be expected to exert an influence on the first director's judgment when voting on the transaction.

10-3863. Members' action; definition

A. Members' action respecting a transaction is effective for purposes of section 10-3861, subsection B, paragraph 2 if a majority of the votes entitled to be cast by the holders of all qualified membership interests was cast in favor of the transaction after all of the following:

1. Notice to members describing the director's conflicting interest transaction.

2. Provision of the information referred to in subsection C of this section.

3. Required disclosure to the members who voted on the transaction, to the extent the information was not known by them.

B. A majority of the votes entitled to be cast by the holders of all qualified membership interests is a quorum for the purposes of action that complies with this section. Subject to subsections C and D of this section, members' action that otherwise complies with this section is not affected by the presence of members or the voting of membership interests that are not qualified membership interests.

C. For purposes of compliance with subsection A of this section, a director who has a conflicting interest respecting the transaction shall inform, before the members' vote, the secretary, or other officer or agent of the corporation authorized to tabulate votes, of the number and the identity of persons holding or controlling the vote of all membership interests that the director knows are beneficially owned, or the voting of which is controlled, by the director or by a related person of the director, or both.

D. If a member's vote does not comply with subsection A of this section solely because of a failure of a director to comply with subsection C of this section and if the director establishes that his failure did not determine and was not intended by him to influence the outcome of the vote, the court, with or without further proceedings respecting section 10-3861, subsection B, paragraph 3, may take such action, respecting the transaction and the director and give such effect, if any, to the members' vote, as it considers appropriate in the circumstances.

E. For purposes of this section, " qualified membership interests" means any membership interests entitled to vote with respect to the director's conflicting interest transaction except membership interests that, to the knowledge, before the vote, of the secretary or other officer or agent of the corporation authorized to tabulate votes, are beneficially owned, or the voting of which is controlled, by a director who has a conflicting interest respecting the transaction or by a related person of the director, or both.

10-3864. Conflict of interest policy; exceptions

A. The board of directors of a corporation shall adopt a policy regarding transactions between the corporation and interested persons, including the sale, lease or exchange of property to or from interested persons and the corporation, the lending or borrowing of monies to or from interested persons by the corporation or the payment of compensation by the corporation for services provided by interested persons. For the purposes of this subsection, " interested person" means an officer or director of a corporation or any other corporation, firm, association or entity in which an officer or director of a corporation is a member, officer or director or has a financial interest.

B. The requirements of this section do not apply to any of the following:

1. A corporation that had assets at the end of its last fiscal year with a book value of less than ten million dollars, net of accumulated depreciation, or had gross receipts or revenues of less than two million dollars in its last fiscal year.

2. A corporation that offers goods or services only to members who are entitled to vote for its board of directors.

3. A corporation organized for religious purposes that does not have, as a substantial portion of its business, the offering of goods or services on a regular basis to the public for remuneration.

4. A corporation organized by or on behalf of the United States, this state, a political subdivision of this state or an agency or instrumentality of such a governmental entity.

5. A hospital, medical, dental or optometric service corporation licensed pursuant to title 20, chapter 4, article 3.

C. For the purposes of subsection B, paragraph 3:

1. Goods and services include medical, hospital, dental or counseling or social services offered on a regular basis to the public for remuneration.

2. A corporation organized for religious purposes includes a corporation or foreign corporation that controls or is controlled directly or indirectly by a corporation or foreign corporation organized for religious purposes.

D. The exemption provided by subsection B, paragraph 4 does not apply to a corporation that provides services to or operates assets of the governmental entity pursuant to a lease or contract.

10-11001. Authority to amend

A. A corporation may amend its articles of incorporation at any time to add or change a provision that is required or permitted in the articles of incorporation or to delete a provision that is not required in the articles of incorporation. Whether a provision is required or permitted in the articles of incorporation is determined as of the effective date of the amendment.

B. A member of the corporation does not have a vested property right resulting from any provision in the articles of incorporation, including provisions relating to management, control or purpose of duration of the corporation.

10-11002. Amendment by board of directors

A. If a corporation has members who are otherwise entitled to vote on amendments to the corporation's articles, then unless the articles of incorporation provide otherwise, a corporation's board of directors may adopt one or more amendments to the corporation's articles without member approval to either:

1. Extend the duration of the corporation if it was incorporated at a time when limited duration was required by law.

2. Delete the names and addresses of the initial directors.

3. Delete the name and address of the initial statutory agent or known place of business, if a statement of change is on file with the commission.

4. Change the corporate name by substituting the word " corporation" , " incorporated" , " company" , " limited" , " association" , " society" , or the abbreviation " corp." , " inc." , " co." , " ltd." , " assn." or " socy." for a similar word or abbreviation in the name, or by adding, deleting or changing a geographical attribution to the name.

5. Make any other change expressly permitted by chapters 24 through 40 of this title or the articles of incorporation to be made by director action.

B. If a corporation has no members or if no members are entitled to vote on the proposed amendment, the board of directors may adopt one or more amendments to the corporation's articles of incorporation.

C. Adoption of an amendment pursuant to this section requires the approval in writing by any person or persons whose approval is required pursuant to section 10-11030 for an amendment to the articles of incorporation or bylaws.

10-11003. Amendment by board of directors and members

A. The following apply to amendments to the articles of incorporation by the board of directors and the members, if there are members entitled to vote on the amendment:

1. A corporation's board of directors may propose one or more amendments to the articles of incorporation for submission to the members.

2. For the amendment to be adopted all of the following shall have occurred:

   a) The board of directors shall recommend the amendment to the members unless the board of directors determines that because of conflict of interest or other special circumstances it should make no recommendation and communicates the basis for that determination to the members with the amendment.

   b) The members entitled to vote on the amendment shall approve the amendment as provided by paragraph 5 of this subsection.

   c) Each person whose approval is required by the articles of incorporation as authorized by section 10-11030 for an amendment to the articles of incorporation or bylaws shall approve the amendment in writing.

3. The board of directors may condition its submission of the proposed amendment on any basis.

4. The corporation shall notify each member entitled to vote of the proposed members' meeting in accordance with section 10-3705. The notice of meeting shall also state that the purpose or one of the purposes of the meeting is to consider the proposed amendment and shall contain or be accompanied by a copy or summary of the amendment.

5. Unless chapters 24 through 40 of this title, the articles of incorporation or the board of directors acting pursuant to paragraph 3 of this subsection requires a greater vote or voting by class, the amendment to be adopted shall be approved by two-thirds of the votes cast or a majority of the voting power, whichever is less.

B. The following apply to amendments to the articles of incorporation by the members, if there are members:

1. If the articles of incorporation expressly permit, the members may propose amendments to the articles of incorporation. If so permitted, the articles of incorporation shall set forth procedures for adopting member initiated amendments, including the percentage of voting power and method of notice required to propose an amendment and the responsibility for calling a member meeting to consider the amendment.

2. For the amendment to be adopted, all of the following shall have occurred:

   a) The members entitled to vote on the amendment shall approve the amendment as provided in paragraph 4 of this subsection.

   b) The corporation shall notify each member in accordance with subsection A, paragraph 4 of this section.

   c) Each person whose approval is required by the articles of incorporation as authorized by section 10-11030 for an amendment to the articles of incorporation or bylaws shall approve the amendment in writing.

3. The members may condition adoption of the proposed amendment on any basis.

4. Unless chapters 24 through 40 of this title, the articles of incorporation or the members acting pursuant to paragraph 3 of this subsection require a greater vote or voting by class, the amendment to be adopted shall be approved by two-thirds of the votes cast or a majority of the voting power, whichever is less.

10-11004. Class voting by members on amendments

The members of a class of a corporation are entitled to vote as a class on a proposed amendment to the articles of incorporation only if a class vote is provided for in the articles of incorporation or bylaws.

10-11006. Articles of amendment

A. A corporation amending its articles of incorporation shall deliver to the commission for filing articles of amendment setting forth:

1. The name of the corporation.

2. The text of each amendment adopted.

3. The date of each amendment's adoption.

4. A statement that the amendment was duly adopted by act of the members or act of the board of directors and, if applicable, with the approval required pursuant to section 10-11030.

B. Within sixty days after the commission approves the filing, a copy of the articles of amendment shall be published. An affidavit evidencing the publication may be filed with the commission.

10-11007. Restated articles of incorporation

A. A corporation's board of directors may restate its articles of incorporation at any time with or without approval by the members or any other person.

B. The restatement may include one or more amendments to the articles of incorporation. If the restatement includes an amendment requiring approval by the members or any other person, it shall be adopted as provided in section 10-11003.

C. If the board of directors submits a restatement for member action, the corporation shall notify each member entitled to vote of the proposed membership meeting in writing in accordance with section 10-3705. The notice shall also state that the purpose or one of the purposes of the meeting is to consider the proposed restatement and shall contain or be accompanied by a copy or summary of the restatement that identifies any amendment or other change it would make in the articles.

D. If the board of directors submits a restatement for member action by written ballot or written consent, the material that solicits the approval shall contain or be accompanied by a copy or summary of the restatement that also identifies any amendment or other change it would make in the articles of incorporation.

E. A corporation restating its articles of incorporation shall deliver to the commission for filing articles of restatement setting forth the name of the corporation and the text of the restated articles of incorporation together with a certificate setting forth:

1. Whether the restatement contains an amendment to the articles requiring approval by any other person other than the board of directors and, if it does not, that the board of directors adopted the restatement.

2. If the restatement contains an amendment to the articles requiring approval by the members, a statement that such approval was obtained.

3. If the restatement contains an amendment to the articles requiring approval by a person whose approval is required pursuant to section 10-11030, a statement that such approval was obtained.

F. Duly adopted restated articles of incorporation supersede the original articles of incorporation and all amendments to them.

G. The commission may certify restated articles of incorporation, as the articles of incorporation currently in effect, without including the certificate information required by subsection E of this section.

H. Within sixty days after the commission approves the filing, a copy of the articles of restatement shall be published. An affidavit evidencing the publication may be filed with the commission.

10-11008. Amendment pursuant to reorganization

A. A corporation's articles may be amended pursuant to this section without action by the board of directors or members or approval required pursuant to section 10-11030 to carry out a plan of reorganization ordered or decreed by a court of competent jurisdiction under a federal statute or a statute of this state if the articles of incorporation after amendment contain only provisions required or permitted by section 10-3202.

B. Before the date of entry of a final decree in the reorganization proceeding, the individual or individuals designated by the court plan shall deliver to the commission articles of amendment setting forth all of the following:

1. The name of the corporation.

2. The text of each amendment contained in the plan of reorganization.

3. The date of the court's order or decree confirming the plan of reorganization containing the articles of amendment.

4. The title of the reorganization proceeding in which the order or decree was entered.

5. A statement that the court had jurisdiction of the proceeding under federal or state statute.

C. This section does not apply after entry of a final decree in the reorganization proceeding even though the court retains jurisdiction of the proceeding for limited purposes unrelated to consummation of the reorganization plan.

D. Within sixty days after the commission approves the filing, a copy of the articles of amendment shall be published. An affidavit evidencing the publication may be filed with the commission.

10-11009.   Effect of amendment and restatement

An amendment to the articles of incorporation does not affect a cause of action existing against or in favor of the corporation, a proceeding to which the corporation is a party, any requirement or limitation imposed on the corporation or any property held by it by virtue of any trust on which that property is held by the corporation or the existing rights of persons other than members of the corporation. An amendment changing a corporation's name does not abate a proceeding brought by or against the corporation in its former name.

10-11020. Amendment by board of directors

A. If a corporation has no members, its board of directors may adopt one or more amendments to the corporation's bylaws.

B. The adoption of an amendment pursuant to this section shall require the approval in writing by any person or persons whose approval is required pursuant to section 10-11030.

10-11021. Amendment by board of directors or members

If the articles of incorporation or the bylaws require that an amendment to or repeal of the corporation's bylaws be submitted to the members, the procedures set forth in section 10-11003 shall apply.

10-11022. Class voting by members on amendments

The members of a class of a corporation are entitled to vote as a class on a proposed amendment to the bylaws only if a class vote is provided for in the articles of incorporation or bylaws.

10-11023. Bylaw increasing quorum or voting requirement for members

A. If authorized by the articles of incorporation, members may adopt or amend a bylaw that fixes a greater quorum or voting requirement for members, or of classes of members, than is required by chapters 24 through 40 of this title. The adoption or amendment of a bylaw that adds, changes or deletes a greater quorum or voting requirement for members shall meet the same quorum requirement and shall be adopted by the same vote and classes of members required to take action under the quorum and voting requirement then in effect or proposed to be adopted, whichever is greater.

B. A bylaw that fixes a greater quorum or voting requirement for members under subsection A shall not be adopted, amended or repealed by the board of directors.

10-11024. Bylaw increasing quorum or voting for directors

A. A bylaw that fixes a greater quorum or voting requirement for the board of directors may be amended or repealed as follows:

  1. If originally adopted by the members, only by the members.

  2. If originally adopted by the board of directors, either by the members or by the board of directors.

B. A bylaw that is adopted or amended by the members and that fixes a greater quorum or voting requirement for the board of directors may provide that it may be amended or repealed only by a specified vote of either the members or the board of directors.

C. Action by the board of directors under subsection A, paragraph 2 to adopt or amend a bylaw that changes the quorum or voting requirement for the board of directors shall meet the same quorum requirement and shall be adopted by the same vote required to take action under the quorum and voting requirement then in effect or proposed to be adopted, whichever is greater.

10-11030. Approval by third persons

The articles of incorporation may require a specified person or persons other than the board of directors to approve in writing any amendment to the articles of incorporation or bylaws and, unless the articles of incorporation or bylaws otherwise provide, that article provision may only be amended with the approval in writing of the specified person or persons.

10-11031. Amendment terminating members or redeeming or canceling memberships

A. Any amendment to the articles of incorporation or bylaws of a corporation that terminates all members or any class of members or redeems or cancels all memberships or any class of memberships shall be adopted in accordance with section 10-11002, 10-11003, 10-11020 or 10-11021, as applicable, and this section.

B. The members shall approve any amendment described in subsection A of this section by two-thirds of the votes cast by each class.

C. The provisions of section 10-3621 do not apply to any amendment described in subsection A of this section.

10-11301. Prohibited distributions

Except as authorized by section 10-11302, a corporation shall not make any distributions.

10-11302. Authorized distributions

A. A corporation may purchase its memberships if after the purchase is completed both:

1. The corporation would be able to pay its debts as the debts become due in the usual course of its activities.

2. The corporation's total assets would at least equal the sum of its total liabilities.

B. A corporation may make distributions on dissolution that conform to chapter 37 of this title.

C. Corporation may make distributions to members who are domestic or foreign nonprofit corporations if after the distribution is made both:

1. The corporation would be able to pay its debts as the debts become due in the usual course of its activities.

2. The corporation's total assets would at least equal the sum of its total liabilities.

10-11601. Corporate records

A. A corporation shall keep as permanent records minutes of all meetings of its members and board of directors, a record of all actions taken by the members or board of directors without a meeting and a record of all actions taken by a committee of the board of directors on behalf of the corporation.

B. A corporation shall maintain appropriate accounting records.

C. A corporation or its agent shall maintain a record of its members in a form that permits preparation of a list of the names and addresses of all members and in alphabetical order by class of membership showing the number of votes each member is entitled to cast and the class of memberships held by each member.

D. A corporation shall maintain its records in written form or in another form capable of conversion into written form within a reasonable time.

E. A corporation shall keep a copy of all of the following records at its principal office, at its known place of business or at the office of its statutory agent:

1. Its articles or restated articles of incorporation and all amendments to them currently in effect.

2. Its bylaws or restated bylaws and all amendments to them currently in effect.

3. Resolutions adopted by its board of directors relating to the characteristics, qualifications, rights, limitations and obligations of members or any class or category of members.

4. The minutes of all members' meetings and records of all actions taken by members without a meeting for the past three years.

5. All written communications to members generally within the past three years, including the financial statements furnished for the past three years under section 10-11620.

6. A list of the names and business addresses of its current directors and officers.

7. Its most recent annual report delivered to the commission under section 10-11622.

8. An agreement among members under section 10-3732.

F. Notwithstanding this chapter, a condominium association shall comply with title 33, chapter 9 and a planned community association shall comply with title 33, chapter 16 to the extent that this chapter is inconsistent with title 33, chapters 9 and 16.

10-11602. Inspection of records by members; applicability

A. Subject to subsections E and F of this section, any member who has been a member of record at least six months immediately preceding its demand is entitled to inspect and copy any of the records of the corporation described in section 10-11601, subsection E during regular business hours at the corporation's principal office, if the member gives the corporation written notice of its demand as provided in section 10-3141 at least five business days before the date on which the member wishes to inspect and copy.

B. Subject to subsections E and F of this section, a member who has been a member of record at least six months immediately preceding its demand is entitled to inspect and copy any of the following records of the corporation during regular business hours at a reasonable location specified by the corporation, if the member meets the requirements of subsection C of this section and gives the corporation written notice of its demand as provided in section 10-3141 at least five business days before the date on which the member wishes to inspect and copy the following:

1. Excerpts from any records required to be maintained under section 10-11601, subsection A, to the extent not subject to inspection under subsection A of this section.

2. Accounting records of the corporation.

3. Subject to section 10-11605, the membership list described in section 10-11601, subsection C.

4. The corporation's most recent financial statements showing in reasonable detail its assets and liabilities and the results of its operations.

C. A member may inspect and copy the records identified in subsection B of this section only if the following conditions are met:

1. The member's demand is made in good faith and for a proper purpose.

2. The member describes with reasonable particularity the member's purpose and the records the member desires to inspect.

3. The records are directly connected with the member's purpose.

D. This section does not affect either:

1. The right of a member to inspect records under section 10-3720 or, if the member is in litigation with the corporation, to the same extent as any other litigant.

2. The power of a court, independently of chapters 24 through 40 of this title, to compel the production of corporate records for examination on proof by a member of proper purpose.

E. The articles of incorporation or bylaws of a corporation organized primarily for religious purposes may limit or abolish the right of a member under this section to inspect and copy any corporate record.

F. Unless the board of directors has provided express permission to the member, a member of a corporation that is a rural electric cooperative is not entitled to inspect or copy any records, documents or other materials that are maintained by or in the possession of the corporation and that relate to any of the following:

1. Personnel matters or a person's medical records.

2. Communications between an attorney for the corporation and the corporation.

3. Pending or contemplated litigation.

4. Pending or contemplated matters relating to enforcement of the corporation's documents or rules.

G. This section does not apply to any corporation that is a condominium as defined in section 33-1202 or a planned community as defined in section 33-1802.

H. This section does not apply to timeshare plans or associations that are subject to title 33, chapter 20.

10-11603. Scope of inspection rights; charge

A. A member's agent or attorney has the same inspection and copying rights as the member the agent or attorney represents.

B. The right to copy records under section 10-11602 includes, if reasonable, the right to receive copies made by photographic, xerographic or other means.

C. The corporation may impose a reasonable charge covering the costs of labor and material for copies of any documents provided to the member. The charge shall not exceed the estimated cost of production or reproduction of the records.

D. The corporation may comply with a member's demand to inspect the record of members under section 10-11602, subsection B, paragraph 3 by providing the member with a list of the corporation's members that was compiled no earlier than the date of the member's demand.

10-11604. Court ordered inspection

A. If a corporation does not allow a member who complies with section 10-11602, subsection A to inspect and copy any records required by that subsection to be available for inspection, the court in the county where the corporation's known place of business is located may summarily order inspection and copying of the records demanded at the corporation's expense upon application of the member.

B. If a corporation does not allow within a reasonable time a member to inspect and copy any other record, the member who complies with section 10-11602, subsections B and C may apply to the court in the county where the corporation's known place of business is located for an order to permit inspection and copying of the records demanded. The court shall dispose of an application under this subsection on an expedited basis.

C. If the court orders inspection and copying of the records demanded, it shall also order the corporation to pay the member's costs, including reasonable attorney fees, incurred to obtain the order, unless the corporation proves that it refused inspection in good faith because it had a reasonable basis for doubt about the right of the member to inspect the records demanded. The court may order a member to pay all or a portion of the corporation's costs, including reasonable attorney fees, if the demand to inspect is denied in whole or in material part.

D. If the court orders inspection and copying of the records demanded, it may impose reasonable restrictions on the use or distribution of the records by the demanding member.

10-11605 Limitations on use of membership list; applicability

A. Without the consent of the board of directors, no person may obtain or use a membership list or any part of the membership list for any purpose unrelated to a member's interest as a member.

B. Without the consent of the board of directors, the membership list or any part of the membership list shall not be:

1. Used to solicit money or property, unless the money or property will be used solely to solicit the votes of the members in an election to be held by the corporation.

2. Used for any commercial purpose.

3. Sold to or purchased by any person.

C. This section does not apply to timeshare plans or associations that are subject to title 33, chapter 20.

10-11620. Financial statements for members

A. Except as provided in the articles of incorporation or bylaws of a corporation organized primarily for religious purposes, a corporation on written demand from a member shall furnish that member its latest annual financial statements that may be consolidated or combined statements of the corporation and one or more of its subsidiaries or affiliates, as appropriate, and that include a balance sheet as of the end of the fiscal year and statement of operations for that year. If financial statements are prepared for the corporation on the basis of generally accepted accounting principles, the annual financial statements shall also be prepared on that basis.

B. If the annual financial statements are reported on by a certified public accountant, that report shall accompany them. If not, the statements shall be accompanied by a statement of the president or the person responsible for the corporation's accounting records both:

1. Stating that person's reasonable belief whether the statements were prepared on the basis of generally accepted accounting principles and, if not, describing the basis of preparation.

2. Describing any respects in which the statements were not prepared on a basis of accounting consistent with the statements prepared for the preceding year.

10-11621. Report of indemnification to members

If a corporation indemnifies or advances expenses to a director under sections 10-3851 through 10-3854, the corporation shall report the indemnification or advance in writing to the members with or before the notice of the next meeting of members. Failure to report under this section does not invalidate otherwise valid indemnification.

10-11622. Annual report

A. Each domestic corporation and each foreign corporation authorized to conduct affairs in this state shall deliver to the commission for filing an annual report that sets forth all of the following:

1. The name of the corporation and the state or country under whose law it is incorporated.

2. The address of its known place of business and the name and address of its agent in this state.

3. The address of its principal office.

223

4. The names and business addresses of its directors and principal officers.

5. A brief description of the nature of its activities.

6. Whether or not it has members.

7. A certificate of disclosure containing the information set forth in section 10-3202, subsection D.

8. A statement that all corporate income tax returns required by title 43 have been filed with the department of revenue.

B. The information in the annual report shall be current as of the date the annual report is executed on behalf of the corporation.

C. The annual report for all corporations shall be delivered to the commission for filing, and the annual fee shall be paid on or before the date assigned by the commission. The commission may stagger the annual report filing date for all corporations and adjust the annual fee on a pro rata basis. The corporation shall deliver the annual report to the commission for filing each subsequent year in the anniversary month on the date assigned by the commission. If a corporation is unable to file the annual report required by this section on or before the date prescribed by this section, the corporation may file, but only on or before this date, a written request with the commission for an extension of time, not to exceed six months, in which to file the annual report. The request for an extension of time shall be accompanied by the annual registration fee required by law. After filing the request for an extension of time and on receipt of the annual registration fee, the commission shall grant the request.

D. If an annual report does not contain the information requested by this section, the commission shall promptly notify the reporting domestic or foreign corporation in writing and shall return the report to it for correction. If the report is corrected to contain the information required by this section and delivered to the commission within thirty days after the effective date of notice, it is deemed to be timely filed.

E. Any corporation that is exempt from the requirement of filing an annual report shall deliver annually a certificate of disclosure containing the information set forth in section 10-3202, subsection D, executed by any two executive officers or directors of the corporation on or before May 31. If the certificate is not delivered within ninety days after the due date of the annual report or within ninety days after May 31 in the case of any corporation that is exempt from the requirement of filing an annual report, the commission shall initiate administrative dissolution of that corporation or revoke the application for authority of that corporation in accordance with chapters 24 through 40 of this title.

F. Any corporation that is exempt from the requirement of filing an annual report shall deliver annually a certificate of disclosure that contains the information set forth in section 10-3202, subsection D and that is executed by any two executive officers or directors of the corporation on or before May 31. If the certificate is not delivered within ninety days after the due date of the annual report or within ninety days after May 31 in the case of any corporation that is exempt from the requirement of filing an annual report, the commission shall initiate administrative dissolution of that corporation or revoke the application for authority of that corporation pursuant to chapters 24 through 40 of this title.

10-11701 Application to existing domestic corporations

A. Except as provided in subsection B, chapters 24 through 40 of this title apply to all Arizona corporations that were incorporated under or that were subject to chapter 22 of this title on December 31, 1998.

B. Any existing corporation that was originally organized under the laws of the territory of Arizona may elect to amend or restate its articles of incorporation and retain any previously valid provisions of its articles of incorporation, even if the previously valid provisions of its articles of incorporation are in conflict with any provisions of chapters 24 through 40 of this title. Upon such amendment or restatement, all of the provisions of chapters 24 through 40 of this title which are not specifically in conflict with the amended or restated articles of incorporation shall be applicable to the existing corporations that were originally organized under the laws of the territory of Arizona. The previously valid provisions of its articles of incorporation that are retained shall apply to the existing corporations originally organized under the laws of the territory of Arizona and to all persons contracting or in any manner dealing with the corporation, including its members, subscribers, affiliates, directors, officers and employees.

References and Resources

Disclaimer: These notes, web addresses, etc. are provided as a reference only. The "notes" are those included as footnotes, and the additional resources are other supporting items to be used for your ongoing benefit... to continue your own personal awareness and connections in the realm of HOAs.

NOTES

1. **FIND LAW:**

   http://realestate.findlaw.com/owning-a-home/history-of-homeowners-associations.html

2. **Arizona State Senate Issue Brief**, November 25, Homeowners' Associations

   http://www.azleg.gov/briefs/Senate/HOMEOWNERS'%20ASSOCIATIONS.pdf

3. **Robert Rules of Order** (http://www.rulesonline.com)

4. **HOA Website:** http://www.hoa-sites.com

5. **Property Management:**
   https://www.irem.org/education/learningtoolbox/homeownersassoc

6. **Real Estate Recovery Fund:** A.R.S. 32-2186
   http://www.azleg.gov/ars/32/02186.htm

7. **ADRE Licensing:**
   http://www.azre.gov/Lic/Documents/Original_Licensing_Brochure_2_2015.pdf

8. **Wikipedia:** https://en.wikipedia.org/wiki/Reserve_study

9. **Community Association Institute** (CAI), Best practices, page 18
   http://www.cairf.org/publications/best_practices.aspx

10. **State of California, Dept. of Real Estate, Reserve Study Guidelines for HOAs**
    http://www.dre.ca.gov/files/pdf/re25.pdf

11.**Arizona Landlord Tenant Act**
https://www.azsos.gov/services/public-information/landlord-tenant-acts

OTHER RESOURCES

Arizona Revised Statutes (A.R.S.) § 41-121(12) states the Secretary of State will: "make available to the public, without charge, title 33, chapters 10 and 11 on the secretary of state's website."

Arizona Residential Landlord and Tenant Act

The Arizona Residential Landlord and Tenant Act; Arizona Revised Statutes Title 33, Ch. 10; is available from the Arizona Department of Housing (PDF) and on Arizona's legislative government site.

> https://housing.az.gov/sites/default/files/documents/files/AZ Residential Landlord and Tenant Act - Revised July 3 2015.pdf

> http://www.azleg.gov/arsDetail/?title=33

The Arizona Mobile Home Parks Residential Landlord and Tenant Act

The Arizona Mobile Home Parks Residential Landlord and Tenant Act; Arizona Revised Statutes Title 33, Ch. 11; is available from the Department of Fire, Building and Life Safety.

> http://www.dfbls.az.gov/lta.aspx

HOA-USA

Dedicated to providing resources that promote a better understanding of town home, condominium, and single-family homeowner associations in your state.

> http://www.hoa-usa.com/statelaws/az.aspx

Homeowners Associations Research Guide

> https://web.law.asu.edu/library/RossBlakleyLawLibrary/Research Now/ResearchGuides/HomeownersAssociationsResearchGuide.aspx

Professional Community Association Management

http://www.homeownerresources.com/search-results?search=arizona

Community Associations Network

http://communityassociations.net/arizona-resources/

First Service Residential | HOA Resource Center

Valuable resources for HOA Board members and homeowners to find information and answers about some of the most critical issues and challenging faced by associations throughout the country.

https://www.fsresidential.com/corporate/search?searchtext=arizona&searchmode=anyword

Arizona Association of Community Managers

https://www.aacm.com/

HOA Management and Property Management Services

https://associaonline.com/locations/associa-arizona

MacQueen & Gottlieb, PLC_

A premier real estate boutique law firm handling HOA matters throughout Arizona. For more information, contact Patrick MacQueen, Esq.

http://www.mandglawgroup.com

HOA Corner

Resources for community associations—SRP offers services that can be of value to community managers and homeowners' associations.

http://www.srpnet.com/service/business/hoa.aspx

Practical Advice for Condominium and Homeowners Association Leadership

HOAleader.com will help keep your homeowner or condominium association up-to-date with HOA laws and out of legal trouble . . . prevent and resolve conflicts in your community . . . make HOA management easier . . . save you money, time and headaches . . . and much more!

http://www.hoaleader.com/

Notes from the Authors

WE HOPE YOU find our book to be of help if you are:

1. Looking for property
2. Selling property
3. Managing property
4. Interested in serving on a board/or already serving on a board.

We endeavored to get to the point without wordy elaboration. We always hear "knowledge is power!" And so it is. By understanding the basics for HOAs and the opportunities for upgrading existing HOAs, it will be easier to shine a light on the subject and make good decisions. Living in a community is an important element and component to one's lifestyle. Getting involved in working with neighbors to make everyone's life better and more complete is a wonderful goal. Sharing with likeminded neighbors, or not, offering your talents and experience to mesh with others is a great way to add value to your life. The welcoming willingness and graciousness of the boards and committees extended to you for your participation, is a very positive sign! Hopefully your experience will be a good one and your neighborhood will come together as a model for all HOAs.

In his book, *HOA Syndrome*, Professor Gary Solomon, PhD, speaks of a psychiatric disorder that is manifesting itself as a result of HOAs that are run as dictatorships; where the residents lose their individuality in order to blend and not cause dissention. This book is an interesting read as it calls attention to abuses caused by adult bullying that exists in some communities. This is an extremely important issue not to be taken lightly. Power can corrupt!! The very special traits that make you who you are, when cultivated by a smart and well-run association, can make your homeownership experience a wonderful one! That is our wish for you!

ABOUT THE AUTHORS

AS A COUPLE, highly qualified to write a key resource on Homeowners Associations (HOAs), Burt and Susan Sweetow are an amazing collective of wisdom, education, and expertise in myriad factors of homeownership. As a team, passionate about HOAs, they are unstoppable! They have worked with Homeowners Associations for decades—working in tandem with homeowners, associations, and property management companies—each experience adding another layer to their belief *it is possible to maximize the benefit of HOAs to ensure peaceful and pleasant communities—if only people will use the knowledge available for them.* HOAs are not simple, and most people are not aware of the various laws and rulings that regulate

them and often don't know where to look. The couple wants to raise awareness and provide a one-stop resource for HOA information and rulings that makes the process of gaining valuable information less difficult for every person who needs it.

Their education and experience are lengthy and impressive: President/Owner/Instructor of the Southwestern School of Real Estate since 1989; Realtors, speakers, trainers and lecturers—always being recognized as the "go-to" for latest trends and issues in the housing industry.

Susan and Burt add an additional layer to home owner association issues with their background and experience as approved mediators for Justice Court and Superior Court—well known for their experience in talking with people in stressful situations to reach positive conclusions.

Burt adds to the couple's mix high-level experience in property and business management for homeowners associations, with a broad skill-set on budgeting, financial planning, operations management, advertising and marketing programs, as well as consulting for apartment building—condominium conversions.

The couple has graced Arizona with their professionalism since 1976, and continues as local residents to share their time and talent with its communities. Susan, a mixed media artist creates work of art that was shown in local galleries, and donated for silent auctions as part of the couple's philanthropic spirit. Burt donated his time to updating Taliesin's archives to computer several years ago. He also computerized cancer records for Scottsdale Health Care as a volunteer. For eight years the couple delivered meals to homebound residents... brightening their day with a cold lunch and hot dinner.

Author's Request for Reviews

If you enjoyed reading *HOAs and All That Jazz!* we would appreciate it if you would help others enjoy the book, too.

LEND IT. This book is lending enabled, so please feel free to share with a friend.

RECOMMEND IT. Please help other readers find the book by recommending it to readers' groups, discussion boards, Goodreads, etc.

REVIEW IT. Please tell others why you liked this book by reviewing it on the site where you purchased it, on your favorite book site, or your own blog. Amazon, being probably the largest distributor of books as the online giant bookstore, makes the review process easy··· log into your Amazon account, search for the book's title, and then click on the hyperlink, *Customer Reviews*. You will be taken to just the right area to post your own review of what you liked about the book and what you feel other readers might experience. Oh, and thank you in advance!

EMAIL US we'd love to hear from you.

burtandsusan@gmail.com

BIBLIOGRAPHY

[1] FIND LAW:
http://realestate.findlaw.com/owning-a-home/history-of-homeowners-associations.html

Paleofuture:
[2] http://paleofuture.gizmodo.com/broadacre-city-frank-lloyd-wrights-unbuilt-suburban-ut-1509433082

[3] Arizona State Senate Issue Brief, November 25, Homeowners'
Associations:
http://www.azleg.gov/briefs/Senate/HOMEOWNERS'%20ASSOCIA
TIONS.pdf

[4] Robert Rules of Order:
http://www.rulesonline.com

[5] HOA Website:
http://www.hoa-sites.com

[6] Property Management:
https://www.irem.org/education/learningtoolbox/homeownersassoc

[7] Real Estate Recovery Fund: A.R.S. 32-2186
http://www.azleg.gov/ars/32/02186.htm

[8] ADRELicensing:
http://www.azre.gov/Lic/Documents/Original_Licensing_Brochure_2
_2015.pdf

[9] Wikipedia:
https://en.wikipedia.org/wiki/Reserve_study

[10] State of California, Dept. of Real Estate, Reserve Study Guidelines
for HOAs:
http://www.dre.ca.gov/files/pdf/re25.pdf

[11] Community Association Institute (CAI), Best practices, page 18
http://www.cairf.org/publications/best_practices.aspx

NOTES

_____

_____

_____

_____

_____

_____

_____

_____

_____

_____

_____

_____

_____

_____

_____

_____

_____

_____

_____

_____

_____

_____

_____

_____

_____

_____

_____

_____

_____

_____

_____

_____

_____

_____

_____

_____

83540122R00144

Made in the USA
San Bernardino, CA
27 July 2018